MEDI

CRUISE PORTS

TRAVEL GUIDE

2024-2025

Discover Top destinations, Cultural Highlights, and Must-Do Shore Excursions for Your Perfect Cruise Experience.

Gina T. Watson

TABLE OF CONTENTS

INTRODUCTION...8

Why Choose a Mediterranean Cruise?.................10

About Mediterranean cruise..............................15

History and Cultural Overview..........................17

CHAPTER 1...21

PLANNING YOUR TRIP................................21

Overview of Major Cruise Lines........................ 21

Choosing the Right Cruise Line......................... 24

Best Time to Cruise the Mediterranean.................. 29

Booking Your Cruise: Tips & Tricks..................... 34

What to Pack for a Mediterranean Cruise................ 39

Onboard Experience: What to Expect.................... 42

Duration of your trip.....................................47

Entry and visa requirements............................. 49

CHAPTER 2...51

ACCOMMODATION......................................51

Different options of Accommodation on a
Mediterranean Cruise....................................51

How to Book Accommodation for a Mediterranean
Cruise..56

CHAPTER 3...60

NAVIGATING MEDITERRANEAN PORTS............. 60

Arrival and Departure Tips..............................60

Transportation Options at Ports.........................63

Currency, Language, and Etiquette Tips................. 67

CHAPTER 4...70

WESTERN MEDITERRANEAN PORTS..............70

Barcelona, Spain... 70

Marseille, France...73

Nice, France...75

Monaco..78

Livorno (Florence/Pisa), Italy......................81

Civitavecchia (Rome), Italy.........................83

Naples, Italy... 86

Palermo, Italy...89

Valletta, Malta.. 91

CHAPTER 5...**94**

**ICONIC PORTS OF THE EASTERN
MEDITERRANEAN**... **94**

Athens (Piraeus), Greece........................... 96

Mykonos, Greece..98

Santorini, Greece....................................... 101

Rhodes, Greece..103

Heraklion (Crete), Greece......................... 106

Dubrovnik, Croatia....................................108

Split, Croatia... 110

Kotor, Montenegro.....................................113

Istanbul, Turkey...115

CHAPTER 6.. **118**

ADRIATIC PORTS..**118**

Venice, Italian..120

Bari, Italy... 123

Koper, Slovenia..125

Zadar, Croatia.. 127

Corfu, Greece... 129

CHAPTER 7.. **132**

AEGEAN AND BLACK SEA PORT.................... **132**

Thessaloniki, Greece..................................133

Kusadasi (Ephesus), Turkey.......................136

Varna, Bulgaria..................138
Odessa, Ukraine.................. 140
Sochi, Russia..................143
CHAPTER 8..................146
ISLAND DESTINATION..................146
Sardinia, Italy.................. 148
Sicily, Italy..................151
Cyprus..................153
Mallorca, Spain..................156
Corsica, France.................. 158
CHAPTER 9..................161
EXCURSIONS AND DAY TRIPS.................. 161
Guided Tours vs. Independent Exploration.............161
Top day trips from key ports..................166
Historical Excursions..................171
CHAPTER 10..................175
LOCAL CUISINE AND DINING EXPERIENCES 175
Mediterranean Food Highlights..................175
CHAPTER 11.................. 181
ITINERARIES.................. 181
7-Day Western Mediterranean Cruise Itinerary...... 181
10-Day Eastern Mediterranean Cruise Itinerary..... 187
CHAPTER 12..................194
PRACTICAL INFORMATION.................. 194
Tips for First-Time Cruisers..................194
Health and Safety.................. 196
Packing Tips.................. 199
Useful Website and Apps..................201
CONCLUSION..................204
MAP..................206

INTRODUCTION

Mediterranean cruise ports are gateways to a region rich in history, culture, and culinary delights. Each port offers a unique blend of old-world charm and modern vibrancy, where ancient ruins sit alongside bustling markets, and picturesque harbors beckon with the promise of new adventures. From the sun-drenched coasts of Spain to the idyllic Greek islands, these ports are more than mere stops on a journey; they are destinations filled with stories, flavors, and unforgettable experiences.

If you're holding this guide, you're likely on the brink of an incredible journey through one of the most captivating regions in the world. And I'm thrilled to share with you the treasures and hidden gems that await you along the Mediterranean cruise ports.

My own love affair with the Mediterranean began years ago when I took my first cruise through this enchanting region. I still remember the thrill of arriving in Barcelona, where the lively street performers of La Rambla set the stage for an unforgettable adventure. From the cobblestone streets of Rome to the sun-soaked shores of Mykonos, each port offered its unique charm and a rich tapestry of experiences. It was this journey that inspired me to dive deeper into the Mediterranean's many facets and share this knowledge with you.

This guide aims to be your comprehensive resource, whether you're planning your trip or already on board. We'll start by exploring the fundamentals of

Mediterranean cruising, including tips on choosing the right cruise line, understanding entry and visa requirements, and making the most of your time on board. Planning a Mediterranean cruise can be both exciting and overwhelming, so I've included practical advice to help you navigate the process with ease.

Next, we'll delve into each port of call, from bustling cities like Barcelona and Athens to picturesque islands such as Santorini and Mallorca. Each chapter offers a detailed look at what you can expect, including must-see sights, local dining recommendations, and insider tips that I've gathered from my own experiences. I've also included practical information on accommodation options, transport to and from the ports, and the best ways to explore each destination.

But a Mediterranean cruise is more than just port stops; it's about the journey itself. We'll cover a variety of excursions and activities, from historical tours and culinary experiences to adventure sports and relaxing beach days. Whether you're interested in exploring ancient ruins, savoring local cuisine, or simply lounging by the sea, this guide has something for every type of traveler.

As you plan your Mediterranean adventure, I hope this guide will be a trusted companion, helping you to craft an itinerary that's as unique and memorable as the Mediterranean itself. So, let's set sail! Dive into the pages ahead, discover the many wonders of the Mediterranean, and prepare for an experience that will stay with you long after you've returned home. Happy cruising!

Why Choose a Mediterranean Cruise?

Choosing a Mediterranean cruise isn't just about selecting a vacation; it's about immersing yourself in a journey that spans centuries of history, diverse cultures, and breathtaking landscapes. The Mediterranean is a region where the past and present converge in the most captivating ways. From the grandeur of ancient civilizations to the vibrant energy of modern cities, each port offers a new chapter in a story that has been unfolding for thousands of years.

Imagine waking up to the sight of the sun rising over the Aegean Sea, with the ruins of ancient temples dotting the horizon. Later that day, you could be exploring the winding streets of a charming coastal village, where the aroma of freshly baked bread mingles with the scent of the sea. This is the magic of a Mediterranean cruise—every day brings a new adventure, a new discovery, and a deeper connection to the rich tapestry of this region.

Diverse Destinations in One Convenient Itinerary

One of the most compelling reasons to choose a Mediterranean cruise is the sheer variety of destinations you can experience in a single trip. The Mediterranean is a mosaic of cultures, each with its own unique traditions, flavors, and landscapes. In just one cruise, you can explore the historic streets of Rome, the artistic treasures of Florence, the whitewashed villages of the Greek Isles, and the glamorous beaches of the French Riviera.

Cruising allows you to seamlessly transition from one world-renowned destination to another without the hassle of packing and unpacking, or dealing with the logistics of transportation. Your floating hotel takes you from port to port, offering a stress-free way to explore the region. Whether you're fascinated by the history of the Roman Empire, enchanted by the beauty of the Greek islands, or eager to taste the culinary delights of Southern Europe, a Mediterranean cruise offers it all in one itinerary.

A Cruise for Every Traveler

No matter what kind of traveler you are, there's a Mediterranean cruise that's perfect for you. If you're a history buff, you'll relish the opportunity to visit iconic sites like the Acropolis in Athens, the ruins of Pompeii, or the medieval fortresses of Dubrovnik. For food lovers, the Mediterranean is a paradise of fresh, local ingredients and time-honored recipes. Imagine savoring a traditional paella in Spain, indulging in pasta and gelato in Italy, or sampling fresh seafood along the coast of Croatia.

If you're seeking relaxation, the Mediterranean offers some of the most beautiful beaches in the world, from the golden sands of Sardinia to the crystal-clear waters of Mykonos. And for those who crave adventure, the region's diverse landscapes provide endless opportunities for outdoor activities, from hiking the rugged trails of the Cinque Terre to sailing along the Amalfi Coast.

The variety doesn't end there. Mediterranean cruises come in all shapes and sizes, from intimate, luxury yachts that offer a more personalized experience, to large, family-friendly ships packed with amenities and entertainment. Whether you're traveling solo, with a partner, or with the whole family, you'll find a cruise that caters to your needs and interests.

Effortless Exploration with a Rich Cultural Experience

One of the greatest advantages of cruising the Mediterranean is the ease with which you can explore multiple countries, cultures, and languages. A Mediterranean cruise offers a truly international experience, often visiting several countries in a single voyage. You could be sipping coffee in a café in Barcelona one day, strolling through a bustling market in Istanbul the next, and watching a sunset over the caldera in Santorini by the end of the week.

Cruising simplifies the logistics of traveling through such a diverse region. There's no need to worry about the complexities of border crossings, currency exchanges, or language barriers—your cruise ship handles all of that for you. This convenience allows you to focus on what really matters: immersing yourself in the culture, history, and beauty of each destination.

And while the convenience of a cruise is undeniable, it doesn't mean you'll miss out on authentic cultural experiences. On the contrary, Mediterranean ports are known for their rich cultural offerings, from world-class museums and historic landmarks to vibrant local markets and traditional festivals. Many cruises offer shore excursions that are carefully curated to give you an in-depth look at the local culture, whether that means visiting a family-owned vineyard in Provence, taking a cooking class in Tuscany, or exploring the ancient ruins of Ephesus with a knowledgeable guide.

Unmatched Scenic Beauty

The Mediterranean is renowned for its stunning natural beauty, and a cruise allows you to experience it from a unique vantage point. As you sail from one port to the next, you'll be treated to panoramic views of sun-drenched coastlines, dramatic cliffs, and sparkling turquoise waters. The Mediterranean is a place where the sea meets the sky in a perfect harmony of colors, where rugged mountains plunge into the ocean, and where every sunset seems more breathtaking than the last.

From the serene beauty of the Greek islands to the lush greenery of the Italian Riviera, the Mediterranean is a feast for the senses. And the best part? You can enjoy these views from the comfort of your ship, whether you're relaxing on the deck, dining al fresco, or unwinding in your cabin. There's something truly special about watching the world go by as you sail through some of the most beautiful waters on earth.

A Perfect Blend of Relaxation and Adventure

A Mediterranean cruise offers the perfect balance between relaxation and adventure. On one hand, you have the opportunity to explore some of the world's most famous cities and historic sites, delving into the art, architecture, and history that have shaped Western civilization. On the other hand, you can spend your days lounging by the pool, enjoying the amenities of your ship, or simply soaking up the sun on a quiet beach.

This flexibility makes a Mediterranean cruise an ideal choice for travelers who want it all. You can tailor your experience to match your mood—one day you might be climbing the steps of the Parthenon, and the next you could be enjoying a leisurely afternoon in a seaside café. The pace is entirely up to you, and with so many options at your fingertips, you'll never feel rushed or overwhelmed.

Finally, a Mediterranean cruise is about creating memories that will last a lifetime. Whether it's the thrill of exploring a new city, the joy of sharing a meal with loved ones, or the simple pleasure of watching the sun set over the ocean, these are the moments that make a cruise so special. The Mediterranean is a place of timeless beauty and endless wonder, and there's no better way to experience it than from the deck of a cruise ship.

From the first time you step aboard, you'll know you're in for something extraordinary. Each day will bring new sights, sounds, and experiences that will stay with you long after your cruise is over. And as you look back on your journey, you'll remember not just the places you visited, but the feeling of discovery, adventure, and connection that only a Mediterranean cruise can offer.

About Mediterranean cruise

Mediterranean cruise ports are some of the most beautiful and exciting destinations you can visit. Each port offers its own unique charm, history, and experiences. As your ship docks at these incredible locations, you'll find a world of adventure waiting for you.

Starting with Barcelona, Spain, this city is vibrant and full of life. Its famous La Rambla street is perfect for a leisurely stroll, where you can enjoy street performers and quaint cafes. Don't miss the breathtaking Sagrada Familia, a masterpiece of architecture by Antoni Gaudí. The city's food markets, like La Boqueria, are a sensory delight with their colorful produce and delicious tapas.

Next, let's sail to Marseille, France. This port city is known for its historic Old Port, where you can watch the boats and sample fresh seafood. The Basilique Notre-Dame de la Garde offers stunning views of the city and the Mediterranean Sea. Wander through the charming streets of Le Panier, the oldest neighborhood in Marseille, filled with artistic vibes and cozy shops.

In Italy, Rome is a must-visit port. The city is a treasure trove of ancient history, from the awe-inspiring Colosseum to the Roman Forum. The Vatican City, with its magnificent St. Peter's Basilica and the Sistine Chapel, is another highlight. After exploring, relax with a slice of authentic pizza or a plate of pasta at a local trattoria.

Florence, also in Italy, is a beautiful city renowned for its art and architecture. The Uffizi Gallery houses masterpieces by Michelangelo and Leonardo da Vinci. Don't forget to visit the iconic Duomo and take a stroll across the historic Ponte Vecchio bridge. The Tuscan countryside surrounding Florence offers picturesque landscapes and delicious cuisine.

The Greek islands are another gem of the Mediterranean. In Santorini, the white-washed houses with blue domes create a postcard-perfect scene. The sunsets here are legendary, best enjoyed with a glass of local wine. The island's fresh seafood, such as grilled octopus, is a culinary delight. Mykonos, another Greek island, is known for its lively nightlife and beautiful beaches.

Istanbul, Turkey, is where East meets West. The city's skyline is dotted with magnificent mosques, including the iconic Hagia Sophia and the Blue Mosque. The bustling Grand Bazaar is a shopper's paradise with its endless stalls of spices, jewelry, and textiles. Turkish cuisine, with its flavorful kebabs and sweet baklava, is not to be missed.

In Croatia, Dubrovnik is a stunning port city with its well-preserved medieval walls and crystal-clear waters. Walking along the city walls offers panoramic views of the Adriatic Sea. The old town is a maze of narrow streets filled with history and charm. Seafood lovers will enjoy the fresh catches served in the local restaurants.

Another enchanting destination is Malta. Valletta, the capital, is a UNESCO World Heritage site known for its rich history and beautiful architecture. The city's narrow streets are lined with baroque buildings, and the Grand

Harbour is a sight to behold. Maltese cuisine, influenced by various cultures, offers delicious dishes like rabbit stew and pastizzi, a savory pastry.

Let's not forget about Morocco. Casablanca, with its blend of modern and traditional, offers a unique experience. The Hassan II Mosque is an architectural marvel located right on the coast. Exploring the local souks, or markets, gives you a taste of Moroccan life with their vibrant colors and enticing aromas. Tagines, couscous, and mint tea are culinary highlights you must try.

Mediterranean cruise ports are more than just places to visit; they are experiences to cherish. Each port offers its own slice of history, culture, and cuisine. From the lively streets of Barcelona to the serene beaches of Santorini, the Mediterranean is a region rich in diversity and beauty. Whether you're exploring ancient ruins, savoring local dishes, or simply soaking in the stunning views, every port has something special to offer. Get ready to create unforgettable memories as you sail through the heart of the Mediterranean.

History and Cultural Overview

The Mediterranean region is like a living history book, filled with stories from ancient times and rich cultural traditions. Here's a simple and easy guide to understanding the history and culture of this fascinating area.

The Mediterranean has been a crossroads of civilizations for thousands of years. It's where Europe, Africa, and

Asia meet, making it a melting pot of cultures, languages, and traditions. Early on, ancient civilizations such as the Egyptians, Greeks, and Romans made their mark here. The Mediterranean Sea was crucial for trade and travel, connecting these cultures and allowing them to share ideas and goods.

In ancient Greece, city-states like Athens and Sparta were famous for their contributions to philosophy, politics, and art. Think of the ancient ruins you might visit, like the Parthenon in Athens. This was a place where philosophers like Socrates and Plato shared their ideas, shaping the foundation of Western thought.

Then came the Romans, who built an extensive empire around the Mediterranean. The Romans were incredible engineers and architects, leaving behind impressive structures like the Colosseum in Rome and the aqueducts that supplied water to their cities. Their influence is still seen today in many aspects of Western culture and government.

After the fall of the Roman Empire, the Mediterranean saw a mix of different powers and cultures. The Byzantine Empire, the continuation of the Eastern Roman Empire, played a significant role in preserving Greek and Roman knowledge. The spread of Islam also brought new influences, with the Arab world contributing advancements in science, mathematics, and medicine.

The Middle Ages were marked by a blend of cultures in the Mediterranean. Crusaders, traders, and explorers from various parts of Europe traveled to the region, interacting with the diverse societies they encountered. This period saw the rise of important maritime powers like Venice and Genoa, which became centers of trade and culture.

As you explore Mediterranean ports, you'll notice a rich cultural tapestry. Spain, for example, boasts a mix of influences from its Moorish past, seen in architectural marvels like the Alhambra in Granada. France's Mediterranean coast, especially in cities like Marseille, reflects its blend of French, North African, and Middle Eastern influences. Italy, with its cities like Rome and Florence, is known for its Renaissance art and architecture, which continues to captivate visitors.

The Greek islands offer a glimpse into ancient mythology and traditional island life. You'll find remnants of ancient temples and beautiful examples of Greek architecture. The islands also celebrate their heritage through festivals and local traditions, adding a vibrant cultural experience to your visit.

In Turkey, Istanbul stands out as a city where East meets West. The Hagia Sophia and the Blue Mosque are landmarks of Byzantine and Ottoman architecture, showcasing the region's complex history. Turkish culture is rich with traditions, from its bustling bazaars to its flavorful cuisine.

Croatia's Adriatic coast, with cities like Dubrovnik, reflects its medieval history and Venetian influence. The city's well-preserved walls and historic buildings tell the story of its strategic importance during the Middle Ages.

Malta's history is a mix of influences from its strategic location in the Mediterranean. Its architecture and culture reflect its time under the rule of various powers, including the Phoenicians, Romans, and Knights of St. John.

Morocco, although not on the European side of the Mediterranean, is closely connected through its maritime history. Its culture is a mix of Berber, Arab, and French influences, seen in its vibrant markets, architecture, and cuisine.

As you travel through the Mediterranean, you'll see how history has shaped each port and region. The blend of ancient traditions and modern life creates a unique and enriching experience. Exploring the Mediterranean is not just about visiting beautiful places; it's about diving into a rich cultural tapestry that spans thousands of years.

CHAPTER 1
PLANNING YOUR TRIP

Planning a trip to the Mediterranean is like preparing for a grand adventure filled with history, culture, and unforgettable experiences. The Mediterranean, with its crystal-clear waters, sun-drenched coastlines, and rich heritage, offers a diverse array of destinations, each with its own unique charm. To make the most of your journey, it's essential to approach the planning process with care and attention to detail.

Overview of Major Cruise Lines

Exploring the Mediterranean on a cruise is a wonderful way to experience the beauty, culture, and history of this enchanting region. Choosing the right cruise line is essential to ensure you have the best experience. Here's an overview of some of the major cruise lines that operate in the Mediterranean, each offering something unique to travelers.

One of the most popular cruise lines for Mediterranean voyages is Royal Caribbean. Known for its innovative ships and wide range of activities, Royal Caribbean provides an exciting and lively atmosphere. The ships are equipped with rock climbing walls, ice skating rinks, and even surf simulators, making them a great choice for families and adventure seekers. The shore excursions offered by Royal Caribbean are well-organized, allowing you to explore iconic cities like Barcelona, Rome, and Athens with ease.

Another excellent option is Norwegian Cruise Line. Norwegian is famous for its "Freestyle Cruising" concept, which offers a more relaxed and flexible approach to dining and entertainment. There are no fixed dining times or dress codes, giving you the freedom to enjoy your vacation at your own pace. Norwegian's Mediterranean itineraries often include stops in picturesque ports like Santorini, Mykonos, and Dubrovnik, providing a mix of stunning landscapes and cultural experiences.

For those looking for a luxurious experience, Celebrity Cruises is a top choice. Celebrity is known for its elegant ships, exceptional service, and gourmet dining options. The staterooms are spacious and stylish, and the onboard amenities include luxurious spas and upscale lounges. Celebrity Cruises also focuses on providing enriching experiences, with excursions that allow you to delve deeper into the history and culture of Mediterranean destinations such as Florence, Venice, and Istanbul.

MSC Cruises offers a distinctly European flair, with a strong emphasis on Mediterranean destinations. The cruise line is known for its beautifully designed ships, which blend modern amenities with classic Italian style. MSC Cruises often features longer stays in ports, giving you more time to explore. They also offer a variety of excursions that cater to different interests, from historical tours to culinary experiences. Ports of call include Marseille, Naples, and Malta, among others.

Princess Cruises is another well-regarded cruise line in the Mediterranean. Known for its excellent service and well-crafted itineraries, Princess Cruises offers a balanced mix of relaxation and exploration. The ships are equipped with comfortable accommodations, multiple dining options, and a range of entertainment choices. Princess Cruises often visits iconic ports such as Athens, Barcelona, and Rome, providing ample opportunities to see famous landmarks and immerse yourself in local culture.

Carnival Cruise Line is a great option for travelers looking for a fun and lively atmosphere. Carnival is known for its vibrant onboard activities, including water parks, live shows, and themed parties. The cruise line offers affordable options, making it accessible for families and budget-conscious travelers. Mediterranean itineraries with Carnival often include stops in beautiful destinations like Palma de Mallorca, Marseille, and Livorno, offering a mix of beaches, culture, and historical sites.

Costa Cruises, an Italian cruise line, offers an authentic Mediterranean experience. Costa's ships are decorated in a charming European style, and the onboard cuisine often features delicious Italian dishes. The cruise line's itineraries focus heavily on Mediterranean ports, with stops in cities like Rome, Venice, and Barcelona. Costa Cruises also offers a variety of shore excursions, from exploring ancient ruins to enjoying local culinary delights.

Each of these major cruise lines offers unique experiences that will help you make the most of your journey through the Mediterranean.

Choosing the Right Cruise Line

When it comes to planning a Mediterranean cruise, one of the most crucial decisions you'll make is choosing the right cruise line. With so many options available, each offering its own unique blend of experiences, amenities, and itineraries, it's important to find the one that aligns with your personal preferences and travel style. The right cruise line can elevate your journey from a simple vacation to an unforgettable adventure, tailored to your desires.

Luxury vs. Mainstream: What's Your Style?

The first step in choosing the right cruise line is to determine what kind of experience you're looking for. Are you dreaming of a luxurious, all-inclusive escape where every detail is meticulously curated? Or perhaps you're seeking a more casual, family-friendly atmosphere with a wide range of activities to keep everyone entertained? Understanding your travel style is key to narrowing down your options.

Luxury cruise lines, such as Regent Seven Seas, Seabourn, and Silversea, offer an elevated experience with a focus on personalized service, gourmet dining, and elegant accommodations. These ships tend to be smaller, which allows for more intimate experiences and access to less crowded ports. If you're looking to indulge in the finer things in life, with a touch of exclusivity, a luxury cruise line might be the perfect choice.

On the other hand, mainstream cruise lines like Royal Caribbean, Norwegian Cruise Line, and MSC Cruises cater to a broader audience, offering a wide array of amenities and entertainment options. These ships are often larger, with more activities, dining venues, and onboard attractions, making them ideal for families, groups, and first-time cruisers. If you're looking for a lively atmosphere with plenty of options to suit different tastes and interests, a mainstream cruise line could be your best bet.

Consider the Itinerary: What Ports of Call Matter Most?

The Mediterranean is a vast region with countless ports of call, each offering its own unique attractions and experiences. When choosing a cruise line, it's important to consider the itineraries they offer and how they align with your interests. Some cruise lines specialize in certain regions or types of experiences, so it's worth doing your research to find the one that visits the destinations you're most excited about.

For example, if your dream is to explore the historic cities of the Western Mediterranean—think Barcelona, Rome, and Nice—you might want to look at cruise lines like Celebrity Cruises or Princess Cruises, which are known for their well-curated itineraries in this region. If the sun-drenched islands of the Eastern Mediterranean, such as Santorini, Mykonos, and Dubrovnik, are calling your name, you might lean towards a cruise line like Azamara, which often includes overnight stays and in-depth explorations in these stunning locations.

Some cruise lines, like Viking Ocean Cruises, offer immersive cultural experiences, with longer stays in port and more opportunities for shore excursions that delve into the history, art, and traditions of each destination. If you're a traveler who enjoys getting off the beaten path and truly immersing yourself in the local culture, these types of itineraries might be particularly appealing.

Onboard Experience: What Matters to You?

The onboard experience is another critical factor to consider when choosing a cruise line. Each cruise line has its own personality, and the amenities, dining options, entertainment, and activities they offer can vary widely. Think about what's most important to you during your time on board, as this will greatly influence your overall enjoyment of the cruise.

If you're a foodie who loves to explore new flavors, you might be drawn to a cruise line with a strong culinary program, like Oceania Cruises or Windstar Cruises, where gourmet dining is a highlight of the experience. These lines often feature partnerships with renowned chefs, offering cooking classes, wine tastings, and exquisite dining experiences that reflect the rich culinary heritage of the Mediterranean.

For those who enjoy a more active vacation, cruise lines like Royal Caribbean and Norwegian Cruise Line offer a plethora of activities, from rock climbing and surfing to fitness classes and sports courts. Families with children or teens might appreciate the extensive kids' clubs, water parks, and entertainment options available on these larger ships, ensuring that everyone in the family has a fantastic time.

If relaxation and wellness are high on your priority list, consider a cruise line that offers a strong focus on spa and wellness services. Lines like Celebrity Cruises and Seabourn often feature luxurious spas, wellness programs, and even mindfulness retreats, allowing you to unwind and recharge as you sail through the tranquil waters of the Mediterranean.

Budget Considerations: Finding the Right Balance

Your budget will inevitably play a role in your choice of cruise line, but it's important to remember that value isn't just about the price tag—it's about what you get for your money. Some cruise lines may appear more expensive upfront, but they include more in the fare, such as gratuities, drinks, shore excursions, and specialty dining. Understanding what's included and what's extra can help you make a more informed decision and avoid any surprises once you're on board.

Luxury cruise lines, while often pricier, typically offer an all-inclusive experience, which means you won't have to worry about additional costs piling up throughout your trip. For travelers who appreciate the convenience of having everything taken care of, this can be a significant advantage.

Mainstream cruise lines, on the other hand, often have more à la carte pricing, allowing you to tailor your experience to fit your budget. If you're looking for flexibility and don't mind paying for extras like specialty dining, drinks packages, or shore excursions, these lines can offer great value. Additionally, mainstream lines frequently run promotions and discounts, making them accessible to a wider range of travelers.

Having cruised the Mediterranean with various cruise lines over the years, I've come to appreciate the subtle differences that each line offers. My first Mediterranean cruise was with Royal Caribbean, and it was a fantastic introduction to cruising. The energy on board was contagious, with so many activities to choose from, and the itinerary covered all the must-see ports. It was a great option for a first-timer who wanted to see as much as possible without breaking the bank.

Later, I experienced the luxury side of cruising with Seabourn. The difference was night and day—everything from the personalized service to the gourmet dining was exceptional. The smaller ship size allowed us to visit ports that larger ships couldn't access, and the intimate atmosphere on board made it feel like a truly special occasion. If you're celebrating a milestone or simply want to treat yourself, I highly recommend considering a luxury cruise line like Seabourn.

On a more recent trip, I sailed with Viking Ocean Cruises and was impressed by their focus on cultural immersion. The shore excursions were thoughtfully planned, and I appreciated the opportunity to learn more about each destination's history and culture. For travelers who want a deeper understanding of the places they visit, Viking's itineraries are hard to beat.

Remember, this is your journey, and choosing the right cruise line is the first step in ensuring that your Mediterranean cruise is everything you've dreamed it would be. So, take your time, explore your options, and get ready to embark on a voyage that will leave you with memories to last a lifetime.

Best Time to Cruise the Mediterranean

The best time to cruise the Mediterranean is a key part of planning your journey, as the region's climate, crowd levels, and overall atmosphere can vary significantly throughout the year. Each season offers its own unique advantages, and understanding these can help you decide when to embark on your Mediterranean adventure. Whether you're seeking warm, sun-soaked days on the beach, a chance to explore historic sites without the summer crowds, or simply want to experience the region's cultural festivals, there's a perfect time for everyone to cruise the Mediterranean.

Spring (April to June): A Blossoming Experience

Spring is one of the most delightful times to cruise the Mediterranean. From April to June, the region begins to wake up from its winter slumber, and the landscape is transformed with vibrant blooms and lush greenery. The weather is pleasantly warm but not yet scorching, making it ideal for exploring ancient ruins, wandering through charming coastal towns, or enjoying outdoor activities like hiking or cycling.

Another advantage of cruising in spring is that the ports are less crowded than during the peak summer months. This means you can enjoy a more relaxed and authentic experience as you visit iconic destinations like the Amalfi Coast, the Greek Islands, or the French Riviera. You'll also find that local markets and attractions are open and ready to welcome visitors, but without the overwhelming crowds.

Spring is also the season for many cultural festivals and events. For example, in Spain, the famous Feria de Abril in Seville is a vibrant celebration of Andalusian culture, while Greece celebrates Orthodox Easter with various traditional ceremonies and festivities. Cruising during this time allows you to immerse yourself in the local culture and experience these unique events firsthand.

If you're someone who enjoys mild weather, beautiful landscapes, and a slightly slower pace, spring is an excellent time to cruise the Mediterranean. It's a time when the region feels fresh and invigorating, offering a perfect balance between exploration and relaxation.

Summer (July to August): Sun, Sea, and Vibrancy

Summer is the most popular time to cruise the Mediterranean, and for good reason. From July to August, the region is bathed in sunshine, the sea is warm, and the beaches are at their best. This is the time of year when the Mediterranean truly comes alive, with a bustling energy that's perfect for those who love a lively atmosphere.

If you're a sun-seeker who dreams of lounging on pristine beaches, swimming in crystal-clear waters, and enjoying al fresco dining with stunning sea views, summer is the season for you. Ports like Mykonos, Ibiza, and the Amalfi Coast are in full swing, offering a mix of relaxation and excitement. The long, sunny days give you plenty of time to explore, whether it's taking a boat trip to hidden coves, sipping cocktails at a beachside bar, or exploring historic cities in the evening when the temperatures cool down.

However, with the beauty of summer comes the reality of peak season. The Mediterranean's most popular destinations will be bustling with tourists, and you may find that attractions and beaches are crowded. Prices for cruises and shore excursions are generally higher during this time, and you'll need to book well in advance to secure your spot on the most popular itineraries.

Despite the crowds, summer in the Mediterranean offers an unbeatable energy and atmosphere. It's a time of celebration, with music festivals, local feasts, and open-air markets adding to the vibrant scene. If you thrive in the heat and love being part of the action, a summer cruise will provide you with unforgettable memories of sun-drenched days and starry Mediterranean nights.

Autumn (September to October): A Golden Retreat

Autumn is often considered the sweet spot for cruising the Mediterranean. From September to October, the intense heat of summer begins to fade, giving way to cooler, more comfortable temperatures. The sea remains warm, making it perfect for swimming and water activities, while the landscapes take on a golden hue as the leaves start to change.

One of the biggest advantages of cruising in autumn is the reduction in crowds. As the summer holiday season comes to an end, many tourists head home, leaving the ports quieter and more relaxed. This is an ideal time to visit popular destinations like Santorini, Dubrovnik, or the Cinque Terre without feeling overwhelmed by the masses. The cooler weather also makes it more enjoyable to explore cities on foot, hike along coastal trails, or visit archaeological sites.

Autumn is also harvest season in the Mediterranean, and many regions celebrate with food and wine festivals. Imagine sipping wine at a vineyard in Tuscany, sampling fresh olives in Crete, or enjoying a seafood feast in a quaint fishing village. These culinary experiences add a delicious layer to your cruise, allowing you to savor the rich flavors of the Mediterranean as you explore its diverse regions.

For travelers who prefer a more laid-back, intimate experience, autumn is a wonderful time to cruise the Mediterranean. The combination of pleasant weather, fewer crowds, and seasonal festivals creates a perfect backdrop for a relaxing and culturally enriching journey.

Winter (November to March): A Serene Escape

While winter may not be the first season that comes to mind for a Mediterranean cruise, it has its own unique charm, especially for those looking to escape the cold and enjoy a quieter, more serene experience. From November to March, the Mediterranean takes on a different character, with cooler temperatures, fewer tourists, and a more relaxed pace.

Cruising the Mediterranean in winter offers several advantages. For one, you'll find that cruise prices are generally lower, and you can often secure great deals on itineraries that include major cities like Barcelona, Rome, and Athens. The ports are less crowded, allowing you to explore at your own pace, without the long lines and packed streets that are common in other seasons.

Winter is also a great time to visit cultural and historical sites. Museums, galleries, and monuments are less crowded, giving you the chance to fully appreciate the art, history, and architecture of the region. Imagine wandering through the ruins of Pompeii or the ancient streets of Ephesus with only a handful of other visitors, or enjoying a peaceful afternoon at the Vatican Museums without the summer throngs.

While the weather may be cooler, the Mediterranean's mild winter climate still offers plenty of sunny days, especially in the southern regions. And for those who enjoy the festive season, many Mediterranean cities and towns are beautifully decorated for Christmas and New

Year, with charming markets, light displays, and holiday events adding a magical touch to your cruise.

If you're looking for a quiet, reflective escape with a focus on culture and history, a winter cruise in the Mediterranean can be a deeply rewarding experience. It's a time to see the region from a different perspective, away from the hustle and bustle of peak season, and to enjoy the beauty of the Mediterranean in a more intimate and tranquil setting.

Booking Your Cruise: Tips & Tricks

Booking your Mediterranean cruise is an exciting step in planning your trip, but it can also be a bit overwhelming given the range of options and considerations involved. From choosing the right itinerary to securing the best deals, a well-informed approach can make the process smoother and ensure you get the most out of your cruise experience. Here are some detailed tips and tricks to help you book your Mediterranean cruise with confidence and ease.

Start with Research: Know Your Options

Before diving into the booking process, take the time to research and understand the different cruise lines, itineraries, and ship options available. Each cruise line offers a unique experience, so it's important to align your choice with your travel preferences, whether that's luxury, family-friendly, or cultural immersion.

Begin by defining your priorities—whether you want to visit specific ports, enjoy onboard amenities, or have a certain type of itinerary. For example, if exploring ancient ruins and historical sites is a priority, look for cruise lines that focus on routes covering Greece, Italy, and Turkey. If a lively nightlife and beach days are more your style, consider itineraries that include popular destinations like Ibiza or Mykonos.

Read reviews from other travelers, consult travel forums, and check out blogs or travel guides to get a sense of what each cruise line and itinerary offers. This will help you narrow down your choices and ensure that you select a cruise that matches your expectations.

Book Early: Secure the Best Rates and Availability

One of the most effective ways to secure a great deal on your Mediterranean cruise is to book early. Cruise lines often offer early booking discounts and promotions, which can significantly reduce the cost of your trip. Additionally, booking in advance allows you to choose from a wider selection of staterooms and cabins, giving you the best chance of securing your preferred accommodations.

Early booking also means you'll have more flexibility when it comes to selecting your travel dates and itinerary. If you have specific dates in mind or want to travel during a less busy season, booking ahead will increase your chances of availability and ensure that you don't miss out on your preferred options.

Consider a Travel Agent: Expert Assistance

While booking directly through a cruise line's website is an option, working with a travel agent who specializes in cruises can offer numerous benefits. A knowledgeable travel agent can help you navigate the complexities of booking, provide insights into the best itineraries and cruise lines, and even offer exclusive deals and promotions that might not be available to the general public.

Travel agents can also assist with other aspects of your trip, such as arranging pre-cruise accommodations, transfers, and travel insurance. Their expertise can help streamline the booking process and ensure that all the details are taken care of, leaving you with peace of mind as you prepare for your Mediterranean adventure.

Compare Packages: What's Included?

When comparing different cruise options, it's important to look beyond the base price and consider what's included in the package. Cruise fares can vary widely, and what appears to be a great deal at first glance may not be as cost-effective once additional fees and extras are factored in.

Examine what's included in the fare, such as meals, beverages, gratuities, and shore excursions. Some cruise lines offer all-inclusive packages that cover most of these extras, which can provide better value and reduce unexpected costs. Others may have lower base fares but charge separately for things like specialty dining, drinks, and excursions.

Pay attention to the fine print and ensure you understand what is and isn't included. If you're interested in specific activities or amenities, such as a spa treatment or a shore excursion, check whether these are covered or if additional costs will apply.

Flexible Dates: Maximize Your Savings

If your travel dates are flexible, you may be able to take advantage of lower prices and special promotions. Cruise lines often offer discounts for off-peak dates or for sailing during less busy periods. By adjusting your travel dates, you could find significant savings and enjoy a more relaxed and less crowded experience.

Consider traveling during shoulder seasons—typically the months just before or after peak travel periods. For the Mediterranean, this could mean sailing in late spring or early autumn, when the weather is still pleasant but the crowds are thinner and prices are more reasonable.

Check for Promotions and Discounts

Keep an eye out for promotions, discounts, and special offers when booking your Mediterranean cruise. Cruise lines frequently run sales, offer limited-time deals, or provide discounts for specific groups, such as past guests, military personnel, or members of loyalty programs.

Sign up for email newsletters from cruise lines and travel agencies to stay informed about upcoming promotions and exclusive deals. Additionally, follow cruise lines on social media for updates on flash sales and special offers that might not be widely advertised.

From my own experience booking Mediterranean cruises, I've found that thorough research and early planning make a big difference. On one occasion, I booked a cruise during a promotional period and was able to secure a stateroom with a balcony at a fraction of the usual price. It was a fantastic value and provided an incredible experience as I enjoyed scenic views of the Mediterranean from my cabin.

Another time, I worked with a travel agent to plan a more complex itinerary that included multiple ports and a pre-cruise stay in a European city. The agent's expertise was invaluable in arranging all the details and ensuring that everything went smoothly. It was a relief to have someone handle the logistics, allowing me to focus on the excitement of the trip.

Booking your Mediterranean cruise doesn't have to be a daunting task. By researching your options, booking early, considering expert assistance, and being mindful of what's included, you can make an informed decision and secure the best possible experience for your journey. With careful planning and a bit of flexibility, your Mediterranean cruise will be a memorable adventure, filled with breathtaking sights, rich history, and unforgettable experiences.

What to Pack for a Mediterranean Cruise

Packing for a Mediterranean cruise is an exciting yet crucial part of your trip planning. The region's diverse climate and activities demand a well-thought-out wardrobe and the right accessories. Here are a few tips to ensure you're prepared for everything the Mediterranean has to offer, with personal insights to help you pack efficiently and comfortably.

Clothing:
When preparing for your Mediterranean cruise, aim for versatile clothing that suits various activities and weather conditions. The Mediterranean climate is generally warm, but temperatures can vary between day and night, and from one port to another.

For warmer weather, pack lightweight, breathable fabrics like cotton and linen. A mix of short-sleeve shirts, sundresses, and shorts will keep you comfortable during daytime excursions and casual evenings. I've found that a wide-brimmed hat and sunglasses are indispensable, not just for sun protection but also for adding a touch of style. On a past cruise, I enjoyed using a sun hat to keep cool and protect my face during long walks in port cities.

In the cooler evenings or on excursions in more temperate regions, a light jacket or sweater is essential. Even during summer, temperatures can drop, especially near the coast or in higher elevations. I recommend packing a versatile scarf or shawl, which can double as a lightweight blanket on cooler evenings or a cover-up when visiting religious sites.

For spring and autumn cruises, bring long-sleeve shirts, lightweight sweaters, and a medium-weight jacket. The Mediterranean weather can be unpredictable, so layering is key. During a recent autumn cruise, I appreciated having layers to adjust to the changing temperatures throughout the day.

Swimwear and Beachwear:
Given the Mediterranean's stunning beaches and inviting pools, swimwear is a must. Pack at least two swimsuits so you always have a dry one while the other is drying. A cover-up or sarong is also handy for transitioning from the beach to other activities. During one of my cruises, having a stylish sarong made it easy to head from the poolside to lunch at the ship's buffet.

If you plan to participate in water sports or excursions, consider bringing a rash guard or swim shirt for additional sun protection. Many Mediterranean ports feature beautiful beaches, and having your own snorkeling gear can enhance your experience. On a snorkeling trip in Greece, I found having my own gear made the experience more enjoyable and hassle-free.

Footwear:
Comfortable footwear is crucial for a Mediterranean cruise, as you'll likely be walking a lot while exploring various ports. Pack a pair of well-fitting walking shoes or sneakers that offer support and comfort. I learned this the hard way on a trip where I wore unsupportive shoes and ended up with sore feet after a day of sightseeing.

Choosing supportive footwear will help you enjoy your excursions without discomfort.

For evening dinners and more formal events, bring a pair of dress shoes or sandals. Many cruises feature formal nights, so having appropriate footwear is important. However, Mediterranean evenings are often more relaxed than some other regions, so smart-casual attire is typically acceptable. During a recent cruise, I found that a pair of elegant yet comfortable sandals worked perfectly for both casual and semi-formal settings.

Formal Attire:

Depending on your cruise line, you might need formal attire for certain evenings. Pack a couple of formal outfits, such as a cocktail dress or a suit, for any formal nights or special events. Even if your cruise doesn't require formal wear, having a dressy option can be useful for upscale dining or special occasions. I once attended a formal dinner on a cruise and was glad I packed a versatile dress that could be dressed up or down.

Onboard Experience: What to Expect

Embarking on a Mediterranean cruise is not just about the destinations you'll visit; it's also about the journey itself. The onboard experience can significantly enhance your trip, offering a mix of relaxation, entertainment, and culinary delights. Here's what you can expect during your time on board, along with some personal insights to help you make the most of it.

Luxurious Accommodations:
Your stateroom will be your personal retreat during the cruise, and the level of comfort you'll experience is often comparable to a luxury hotel. Cruise lines typically offer a range of accommodations, from cozy interior cabins to spacious suites with private balconies.

If you're looking for a more budget-friendly option, interior cabins are perfectly comfortable, albeit without windows. These rooms are well-appointed and make for a restful night's sleep after a day of exploring. On one of my cruises, I opted for an interior cabin and found it to be a cozy, quiet place to unwind.

For those who prefer a view, oceanview cabins and balcony staterooms provide a glimpse of the sea or the stunning ports as you sail. I've personally enjoyed waking up to the sight of the Mediterranean coastline from a balcony stateroom—it's a truly memorable experience.

Suites offer the ultimate in luxury, with extra space, premium amenities, and sometimes even concierge service. If you're celebrating a special occasion or simply want to indulge, a suite can make your cruise feel even more special.

Dining:

The dining experience on a Mediterranean cruise is a highlight in itself. You can expect a variety of dining options, from casual buffets to elegant à la carte restaurants. One of the pleasures of cruising is the opportunity to sample different cuisines, often inspired by the regions you'll be visiting.

Most ships feature main dining rooms where you can enjoy multi-course meals in a more formal setting. The menus often change daily and offer a selection of international dishes. I've found that trying the local specialties offered on board is a great way to get a taste of the destinations on your itinerary.

Buffet-style dining is available throughout the day, offering a more casual option with a wide range of dishes to suit all tastes. From fresh salads and grilled meats to pasta and desserts, there's always something to satisfy your appetite. On one cruise, I discovered the joy of starting my day with a leisurely breakfast at the buffet, enjoying the sea views as I planned the day's activities.

Many cruise lines also feature specialty restaurants, where you can indulge in gourmet cuisine for an additional fee. Whether you're in the mood for sushi, Italian, or steak, these restaurants offer a more intimate dining experience. I still remember an incredible meal at a Mediterranean-themed restaurant on board, where the flavors perfectly captured the essence of the region.

For those who prefer to dine in the comfort of their stateroom, room service is often available 24/7. On a few occasions, I've enjoyed a quiet dinner on my balcony, watching the sunset over the Mediterranean—a perfect way to end the day.

Entertainment:

Cruise ships are designed to keep you entertained, with a wide range of activities and shows to suit all tastes. Whether you're looking to relax by the pool, catch a Broadway-style show, or try your luck at the casino, there's always something happening on board.

Theaters on cruise ships often host impressive productions, from musicals and comedy shows to acrobatic performances. These shows are professionally produced and offer a level of entertainment that rivals what you'd find on land. I've enjoyed several unforgettable performances during my cruises, including a dazzling tribute to classic rock that had the whole audience on their feet.

For a more relaxed evening, many ships offer live music in lounges and bars. Whether it's a jazz trio, a pianist, or a lively band, there's something for every musical taste. I've found that enjoying a drink while listening to live music is a great way to unwind after a day of exploring.

Daytime activities vary widely and can include everything from cooking classes and wine tastings to dance lessons and art auctions. There are also plenty of opportunities to stay active, with fitness centers, sports courts, and even yoga classes available. During a recent cruise, I took part in a cooking demonstration that introduced me to some traditional Mediterranean dishes, which I later tried to recreate at home.

For those who enjoy gaming, the onboard casino offers a variety of games, from slot machines to poker tables. It's a fun way to spend an evening, even if you're just playing for fun. I've had some memorable nights trying my luck at the blackjack table, even if the house usually wins!

Relaxation and Wellness:

If relaxation is a priority, cruise ships offer numerous options to help you unwind. Most ships have multiple pools and hot tubs, often with stunning views of the ocean. Whether you're looking to take a dip, soak up the sun, or simply relax with a book by the pool, you'll find plenty of space to do so. I've spent many peaceful afternoons lounging by the pool, with the gentle sound of the waves providing the perfect soundtrack.

For a more indulgent experience, the onboard spa offers a range of treatments, from massages and facials to acupuncture and aromatherapy. Spa services are usually an additional cost, but the level of pampering you receive can be well worth it. On one cruise, I treated myself to a hot stone massage after a long day of walking in port, and it was the perfect way to relax and rejuvenate.

Fitness enthusiasts will appreciate the well-equipped gym facilities, which often include state-of-the-art equipment and group fitness classes. Whether you prefer a morning workout or an evening yoga session, staying active on board is easy. I've found that starting the day with a sunrise yoga class is a refreshing way to energize before heading out for a day of exploration.

Kids and Family Activities:

Cruising is a fantastic option for families, with plenty of activities to keep kids entertained. Most cruise lines offer dedicated kids' clubs, where children can enjoy supervised activities tailored to their age group. From arts and crafts to video games and scavenger hunts, there's no shortage of fun for younger travelers.

Teens aren't left out either, with teen lounges and activities designed to appeal to older kids. On family cruises I've been on, the kids' club has been a hit, giving parents some well-deserved downtime while the kids make new friends and enjoy the activities.

Family-friendly entertainment, such as movie nights, poolside games, and themed parties, ensures that everyone has a great time. I've seen families bond over trivia games, participate in dance parties, and enjoy outdoor movie nights under the stars.

Shopping and Souvenirs:

For those who love to shop, cruise ships offer a variety of stores selling everything from duty-free goods to luxury items. Whether you're looking for a special gift, some vacation souvenirs, or just want to treat yourself, there's plenty to browse.

You'll find shops selling clothing, jewelry, cosmetics, and more. Duty-free shopping is also a great opportunity to pick up some luxury items at a lower price. I've picked up some unique souvenirs on board, including local crafts and artwork that remind me of my Mediterranean adventures.

Duration of your trip

Deciding how long to stay at the Mediterranean cruise ports can shape your entire trip. The duration of your visit depends on what you want to see and experience. Whether you're looking for a quick getaway or a more in-depth exploration, understanding the duration of your trip can help you make the most of your time.

If you have only a few days, you can still enjoy a memorable experience. A short visit of three to four days allows you to get a taste of one or two ports. This is ideal if you're interested in seeing a few key sights and soaking up the local atmosphere. With a well-planned itinerary, you can explore a city's top attractions, enjoy a few meals at local restaurants, and perhaps even take a short excursion.

For a more comprehensive experience, consider extending your stay to a week or more. This gives you the chance to delve deeper into each destination, discover hidden gems, and enjoy a more relaxed pace. With a week, you can explore multiple ports, participate in local activities, and truly immerse yourself in the Mediterranean culture. You'll have time to visit popular landmarks, enjoy leisurely meals, and take part in excursions that may require more time.

If you're looking to fully explore the Mediterranean and its diverse offerings, a trip lasting two weeks or more would be ideal. This allows you to visit several ports and experience a wide range of activities and sights. A longer trip gives you the flexibility to visit both well-known destinations and lesser-known spots, enjoy extended shore excursions, and experience the Mediterranean's different regions in more depth. You'll have ample time to appreciate the local customs, try various cuisines, and perhaps even take part in unique cultural events.

When planning the duration of your trip, consider how much time you can comfortably spend away and what you want to achieve during your visit. Think about your interests, whether they lie in historical sites, culinary experiences, or relaxing by the sea. Balancing your time between exploration and relaxation ensures that you enjoy a fulfilling and enjoyable Mediterranean adventure.

The length of your trip should match your travel goals and personal preferences. Whether it's a brief getaway or an extended journey, careful planning will help you make the most of your time in the Mediterranean and create lasting memories.

Entry and visa requirements

When planning a Mediterranean cruise, it's important to understand the entry and visa requirements for the countries you'll be visiting. Knowing these details in advance can help you avoid unexpected expenses and ensure a smooth trip.

First, check if you need a visa for the countries you'll visit. If you're from a country within the European Union, you usually don't need a visa to travel to other EU countries. However, if you're traveling from outside the EU, visa requirements can vary depending on your nationality.

For many Mediterranean countries, especially those in Europe, you'll need a Schengen visa if you plan to visit multiple countries within the Schengen Area. This visa allows you to travel to several countries within this area for up to 90 days within a 180-day period. Applying for a Schengen visa typically requires submitting an application to the consulate or embassy of the country you'll spend the most time in, or if time is equally divided, the country where you'll enter first.

Make sure to apply for your visa well in advance of your trip. Processing times can vary, and applying early helps avoid any last-minute issues. Each country has its own set of requirements for a visa application, but common documents include a valid passport, proof of accommodation, travel insurance, and evidence of sufficient funds for your stay. Check the specific requirements for each country on the embassy's or consulate's website.

If you're on a budget, look for ways to save on visa-related costs. Some countries offer lower fees for certain types of travelers or during specific periods. Additionally, if you're traveling to several countries, you might be able to apply for a multi-entry visa that covers all your destinations, which can be more economical than applying for separate visas.

To keep costs down, gather all necessary documents before you start your visa application. Ensure your passport is valid for at least six months beyond your planned travel dates. Provide all required documentation, such as flight bookings, hotel reservations, and proof of travel insurance. Compare different travel insurance plans to find one that meets the visa requirements and fits your budget. Some insurance providers offer discounted rates for comprehensive coverage, so shopping around can save you money.

If you find the visa process confusing or overwhelming, consider consulting a travel agent or a visa service. They can assist with the application process and ensure you meet all requirements. While this may involve a service fee, it can be worthwhile for the convenience and to avoid potential issues.

By understanding the entry and visa requirements and planning ahead, you can manage your budget more effectively and avoid unexpected costs. Ensure you have all necessary documents and insurance in place to enjoy a smooth and enjoyable Mediterranean cruise.

CHAPTER 2

ACCOMMODATION

Different options of Accommodation on a Mediterranean Cruise

When embarking on a Mediterranean cruise, choosing the right accommodation is an important part of the overall experience. Cruise ships offer a wide variety of cabin options to suit different preferences and budgets, ranging from compact interior rooms to luxurious suites with expansive ocean views. Here's everything you need to know about the accommodation options available on a Mediterranean cruise:

1. Interior Cabins (Inside Cabins)
Interior cabins are the most budget-friendly option on a cruise ship. These rooms are typically located in the interior sections of the ship, meaning they don't have windows or natural light. While they may be smaller and more compact than other cabin types, they are perfect for travelers who plan to spend most of their time exploring the ship or on shore excursions and need a comfortable place to sleep and refresh.

- Pros: Budget-friendly, dark for sleeping, typically quieter.
- Cons: No windows or natural light, smaller in size.

Interior cabins often include standard amenities such as a bed, private bathroom, TV, closet space, and seating area. If you're looking for an affordable way to enjoy a

Mediterranean cruise, this option will allow you to maximize your budget for excursions and onboard activities.

2. Ocean View Cabins (Outside Cabins)
Ocean view cabins offer windows or portholes that allow you to see the sea and outside surroundings. These rooms are usually larger than interior cabins and provide natural light, making them feel more spacious and inviting.

- Pros: Scenic views, natural light, affordable upgrade from interior cabins.
- Cons: Windows are often fixed, so you can't open them for fresh air.

Ocean view cabins are a great middle-ground option if you want to enjoy views of the Mediterranean as you sail without splurging on a balcony cabin. It's especially appealing when cruising through scenic areas like the Greek Isles or the Amalfi Coast, where the sights from your window will add to the experience.

3. Balcony Cabins (Veranda Staterooms)
Balcony cabins, also known as veranda staterooms, provide access to a private balcony where you can step outside to enjoy the fresh sea breeze and views. These cabins are typically larger than interior or ocean view cabins and come with added amenities, making them a popular choice for travelers seeking a more immersive cruise experience.

- Pros: Private outdoor space, fresh air, perfect for scenic cruising.
- Cons: Higher cost compared to inside and ocean view cabins.

Balcony cabins are ideal for travelers who enjoy spending time in their room and want to relax in privacy while taking in the stunning Mediterranean scenery. Whether watching the sunrise over the coast of Italy or enjoying a sunset in the Greek Islands, the added luxury of a balcony enhances the cruise experience.

4. Suites
The most spacious and luxurious accommodations on a cruise ship are suites . They often come with separate living and sleeping areas, larger bathrooms, and private balconies. Many cruise lines also offer suite guests exclusive access to VIP areas, concierge services, and priority boarding and disembarkation.

- Pros: Maximum space and comfort, exclusive services, premium amenities.
- Cons: The most expensive accommodation option.

Suites are perfect for travelers who want to indulge in luxury while cruising the Mediterranean. With added perks like complimentary butler service, exclusive lounges, and fine dining options, staying in a suite ensures an elevated experience with maximum relaxation and personal service.

5. Family Cabins
For families or groups traveling together, many cruise lines offer cabins designed to accommodate multiple

people. These can include connecting rooms, cabins with bunk beds, or even family suites with extra living space and amenities geared towards younger passengers.

- Pros: Designed for larger groups, cost-effective for families, family-friendly amenities.
- Cons: Can be pricier than standard cabins but more affordable than booking multiple rooms.

Family cabins ensure that everyone can stay together comfortably, with plenty of space for children to play and relax. Some ships also offer kids' clubs, family-friendly dining, and entertainment options to make cruising enjoyable for all ages.

6. Accessible Cabins

Many cruise ships also provide accessible cabins for travelers with mobility issues or special needs. These cabins are designed to be larger with more spacious doorways, accessible bathrooms, and other features like grab bars and roll-in showers to ensure comfort and ease of use.

- Pros: Specially designed for accessibility, larger spaces, thoughtful features.
- Cons: Limited availability, so booking early is recommended.

Accessible cabins are an essential option for travelers who need extra space and amenities that accommodate wheelchairs or mobility devices, ensuring a stress-free and comfortable cruise experience.

Things to Consider When Choosing a Cabin
- Budget: Determine how much you're willing to spend on accommodation, keeping in mind that more luxurious cabins come with a higher price tag.
- Views and Outdoor Space: If having a view or balcony is important to you, be prepared to spend more on an ocean view or balcony cabin.
- Location on the Ship: Consider whether you want to be near or far from elevators, dining areas, and entertainment venues. Cabins near the ship's center often experience less motion, making them ideal for those prone to seasickness.
- Cabin Size: If you're traveling as a family or group, a larger room or suite may be necessary to accommodate everyone comfortably.
- Onboard Amenities: Some cabins come with exclusive amenities like access to private areas, butler services, or complimentary room upgrades. Decide which perks are worth the extra cost for you.

By understanding your options and considering your personal preferences, you can select the perfect cabin to enhance your Mediterranean cruise experience. Whether you opt for a simple interior cabin or indulge in a suite with sweeping sea views, your accommodation will play a key role in making your journey both enjoyable and memorable.

How to Book Accommodation for a Mediterranean Cruise

Booking the right accommodation for your Mediterranean cruise involves several steps to ensure you get the best experience for your budget and preferences. Here's a simplified guide to help you through the process:

1. Research and Choose a Cruise Line
Before you book your cabin, research various cruise lines to find one that fits your needs and interests. Different cruise lines offer varying levels of luxury, onboard activities, and itineraries. Look into:

- Cruise Line Reputation: Check reviews and ratings from other travelers.
- Itinerary Options: Ensure the cruise visits the Mediterranean ports you're interested in.
- Ship Facilities: Compare amenities and accommodation options on different ships.

2. Decide on Cabin Type
Determine the type of cabin that best suits your needs:

- Interior Cabin: Best for budget travelers who will spend most of their time off the ship.
- Ocean View Cabin: Offers a window or porthole for natural light and views.
- Balcony Cabin: Includes a private outdoor space for enjoying the scenery.
- Suite: Provides the most space and luxury with added amenities.

- Family or Accessible Cabins: Ideal for larger groups or those with special needs.

3. Check Availability and Pricing
Visit the cruise line's official website or consult with a travel agent to check availability for your preferred travel dates. Compare prices for different cabin types and consider any promotions or discounts that may be available.

4. Review Cabin Location
Consider the location of your cabin on the ship:

- Mid-Ship Cabins: Typically experience less motion and are closer to main facilities.
- Lower Decks: May be quieter and less prone to movement.
- Higher Decks: Often provide better views but can be noisier due to proximity to pools and lounges.

5. Book Your Cabin
You can book your cabin through various methods:

- Directly Through the Cruise Line: Visit the cruise line's website or call their reservations department. Booking directly often provides the most accurate information and access to exclusive offers.
- Travel Agent: A travel agent can help you find the best deals and handle all booking details. They can also provide advice on cabin selection and offer packages or extras.
- Online Travel Agencies: Websites like Expedia, Cruise Critic, or Orbitz offer comparisons across different cruise

lines and can be a good option for finding competitive prices.

6. Consider Extras and Upgrades
Once you've selected your cabin, consider booking additional services and upgrades:

- Dining Options: Some cruise lines offer specialty dining experiences or drink packages.
- Excursions: Pre-book shore excursions to secure spots on popular tours.
- Travel Insurance: Protect your trip with travel insurance that covers cancellations, medical emergencies, and other issues.
- Pre-Cruise Packages: Look for packages that include pre-cruise hotels or airport transfers.

7. Review and Confirm Booking
After booking, review all details to ensure accuracy:

- Booking Confirmation: Check that your cabin type, travel dates, and passenger details are correct.
- Payment: Confirm the payment method and understand the refund and cancellation policies.
- Documents: Ensure you have all necessary travel documents, including passports and visas if required.

8. Prepare for Your Cruise
As your departure date approaches, start preparing for your cruise:

- Packing: Refer to the cruise line's packing list and consider the weather and activities planned.

- Pre-Cruise Check-In: Complete online check-in to expedite your boarding process.
- Excursions and Special Requests: Confirm any pre-booked excursions or special requests with the cruise line.

By following these steps, you'll ensure a smooth booking process and secure the accommodation that best fits your needs for an unforgettable Mediterranean cruise experience.

CHAPTER 3

NAVIGATING MEDITERRANEAN PORTS

Arrival and Departure Tips

Navigating Mediterranean ports can be straightforward if you know what to expect. This section provides essential tips for a smooth arrival and departure at Mediterranean cruise ports.

1. Arrival Tips

- Documentation: Ensure you have all necessary travel documents ready before you disembark. This includes your passport, cruise card, and any required visas. Keep these documents easily accessible but secure.

- Port Customs and Security: Be prepared for security checks at the port. This usually involves screening of bags and possibly a brief inspection of personal items. Follow the port staff's instructions and be patient as these procedures are for your safety.

- Disembarkation Procedures: Listen for announcements on the ship regarding disembarkation procedures. Cruise lines often provide instructions on meeting times, areas, and any necessary forms or requirements. Follow these closely to ensure a smooth process.

- Local Transportation: Research transportation options before arriving. Many ports offer shuttle services, taxis, and public transportation. In some cases, you might need to book transportation in advance, especially for popular or busy ports.

- Port Maps and Information: Grab a port map or information brochure if available. These are often distributed at the dock or can be found at the cruise line's service desk. They provide valuable information about the port area, including transportation options, nearby attractions, and essential services.

2. Departure Tips

- Timing: Arrive at the departure port with plenty of time to spare. This allows for any unexpected delays and ensures a smooth check-in process. The recommended arrival time is usually at least two hours before the ship's departure.

- Check-in Process: Have your cruise card and travel documents ready for inspection at the port. Follow the instructions given by port staff and cruise line representatives to streamline the check-in process.

- Luggage Handling: Most cruises offer luggage handling services where your bags are collected from your cabin and delivered to the port for you. Confirm the details with the cruise line and ensure you adhere to any guidelines provided for luggage tags and timing.

- Final Checks: Before leaving the port, double-check that you have all your belongings and important documents. It's easy to forget personal items, so make a quick review of your cabin and any port area you might have visited.

- Transportation to the Airport or Hotel: If you're continuing your journey to the airport or a hotel, make sure you know the transportation arrangements. Pre-booking a taxi or shuttle service can save time and reduce stress.

3. General Tips

- Local Currency: Have some local currency on hand for port-related expenses. While credit cards are widely accepted, small vendors or transportation services might prefer cash.

- Language: While English is commonly spoken in tourist areas, learning a few basic phrases in the local language can be helpful and appreciated by locals.

- Port Etiquette: Respect local customs and follow any posted rules or guidelines. This includes adhering to designated areas for tourists and being considerate of local residents.

By following these arrival and departure tips, you'll be well-prepared to navigate Mediterranean ports efficiently, allowing you to focus on enjoying your cruise and the exciting destinations ahead.

Transportation Options at Ports

Understanding transportation options at Mediterranean ports will help you explore each destination efficiently and comfortably. Here's a detailed look at the various modes of transport available:

1. Shuttle Services
- Cruise Line Shuttles: Most cruise lines offer shuttle buses that transport passengers from the port to central locations, major attractions, or shopping areas. These shuttles can be convenient and are often included in your cruise package or available for a small fee. Before you arrive, check the cruise line's itinerary or daily schedule for shuttle service information, including pick-up and drop-off points and timings. Shuttles typically operate on a set schedule, so plan your day accordingly to align with these timings.

- Private Shuttles: For a more tailored experience, private shuttle services are a great option. These can be pre-booked online or arranged through local companies at the port. Private shuttles offer flexibility in terms of pick-up and drop-off times and can be a more comfortable choice if traveling with a group or family. Look for reputable providers with positive reviews and ensure they offer the amenities you need.

2. Taxis
- Availability: Taxis are a common and readily available transportation option at most major Mediterranean ports. Taxis can be found at designated stands near the

port terminals. Make sure to use taxis from these stands to avoid unofficial operators who may overcharge.

- Booking and Fare Tips: Official taxis will generally have meters. Confirm that the meter is running or ask for an estimated fare before starting your trip. It's also a good idea to have a rough idea of the fare to your destination to ensure you're not overcharged. For added convenience, consider booking a taxi in advance through apps or local services, especially in busy ports where demand can be high.

3. Public Transportation
- Buses: Local bus services are often available at ports, providing an affordable way to travel to various parts of the city. Bus stops are usually located near the port entrance. Familiarize yourself with bus schedules and routes ahead of time, as they can vary. Public buses are a cost-effective option, but they may not be as frequent or direct as other modes of transportation.

- Trains: In ports like Barcelona, Marseille, and Genoa, train stations are often close to the port. Trains can quickly transport you to nearby cities or regions. Tickets can be purchased at the station or online in advance. Trains are a good option for longer distances and are generally efficient, though checking the schedule and booking in advance is recommended to avoid missing your desired train.

- Trams and Metro: In larger cities, trams and metro systems are well-developed and offer quick access to central areas and major attractions. Metro stations are usually easy to find, and many cities offer multi-day passes or travel cards that can be cost-effective if you plan to use public transport frequently.

4. Car Rentals
- Rental Agencies: Car rental agencies are typically located near major ports or within the city. Renting a car provides flexibility to explore at your own pace and visit locations that might be harder to reach via public transport. Booking a car in advance is advisable, especially during peak tourist seasons, to secure availability and potentially lower rates.

- Parking Considerations: Be aware of local parking regulations and availability. In busy urban areas, parking can be challenging due to narrow streets and limited spaces. Look for parking garages or designated areas to avoid fines or difficulties. Using navigation apps can help you locate parking spots and avoid congested areas.

5. Bicycle and Scooter Rentals
- Availability: Many Mediterranean cities offer bicycle and scooter rentals as an eco-friendly and enjoyable way to explore. Rental stations are often found near the port or in city centers. This option is great for short trips and provides an opportunity to enjoy the local scenery and outdoor environments.

- Safety and Routes: When renting bicycles or scooters, check for dedicated bike lanes or paths to ensure a safe ride. Many cities also offer guided bike tours that can enhance your experience by providing local insights and highlighting key attractions.

6. Walking
- Proximity: For ports close to the city center or major attractions, walking can be a pleasant and practical way to get around. Many ports are pedestrian-friendly, allowing you to explore local shops, restaurants, and landmarks at a leisurely pace.

- Guided Tours: If you prefer a structured experience, consider joining a guided walking tour. These tours provide historical and cultural context, making your visit more informative and engaging.

7. Local Ferries
- Island Hopping: In regions like Greece and Italy, local ferries connect ports with nearby islands and coastal towns. Ferries are a scenic way to travel and can be a great option for exploring multiple destinations in a single day.

- Booking and Schedules: Ferry schedules can vary, so it's important to check timetables in advance. Booking tickets early can help avoid long queues and ensure you get a seat, especially during high season.

By understanding and utilizing these transportation options, you'll be well-prepared to navigate Mediterranean ports effectively. Whether you prefer the convenience of a shuttle, the flexibility of a rental car, or the local charm of public transport, there's a solution to meet every traveler's needs and ensure a smooth and enjoyable port experience.

Currency, Language, and Etiquette Tips

Understanding the currency, language, and local etiquette in Mediterranean ports will enhance your travel experience and help you navigate each destination with ease. Here's what you need to know:

1. Currency

- Currency Overview: The Mediterranean region features several currencies. The Euro (€) is the common currency in countries like Spain, France, Italy, and Greece, while Turkey uses the Turkish Lira (TRY). Malta also uses the Euro, whereas some regions like Monaco use the Euro despite being outside the Eurozone. In certain non-Eurozone countries, like Croatia (where the Croatian Kuna was used until 2023), local currencies might still be in use, so it's important to check the specific country you're visiting.

- Currency Exchange: Currency exchange services are available at airports, port terminals, banks, and exchange bureaus. Currency exchange offices are often found in popular tourist areas. Exchange rates can vary, so it's wise to compare rates before exchanging money. Many ports also have ATMs where you can withdraw local currency using your credit or debit card. Be mindful of potential fees for international transactions.

- Credit and Debit Cards: Credit and debit cards are widely accepted throughout the Mediterranean, especially in urban areas, shops, restaurants, and hotels. Visa and MasterCard are the most commonly accepted, while American Express may be less frequently accepted. It's always a good idea to carry some local cash for smaller purchases or in areas where card payments might not be accepted.

2. Language
- Common Languages: The Mediterranean region is linguistically diverse. In Spain, Spanish is the official language, but regional languages such as Catalan and Basque may also be spoken. In France, French is the official language. Italy uses Italian, while Greece's official language is Greek. In Turkey, Turkish is the primary language spoken. English is commonly understood in major tourist areas, hotels, and restaurants, but learning a few basic phrases in the local language can enhance your interactions.

- Useful Phrases: Knowing some essential phrases in the local language can be helpful:
    - Spanish: "Hola" (Hello), "Gracias" (Thank you), "¿Dónde está...?" (Where is...?)
    - French: "Bonjour" (Hello), "Merci" (Thank you), "Où est...?" (Where is...?)
    - Italian: "Ciao" (Hello), "Grazie" (Thank you), "Dove si trova...?" (Where is...?)
    - Greek: "Γειά σας" (Yia sas - Hello), "Ευχαριστώ" (Efcharistó - Thank you), "Πού είναι...?" (Poú eínai...? - Where is...?)
    - Turkish: "Merhaba" (Hello), "Teşekkür ederim" (Thank you), "Nerede...?" (Where is...?)

3. Etiquette
- Greetings: Each Mediterranean country has its own customs for greetings. In Spain and Italy, a kiss on both

cheeks is common among friends and family, while a handshake is typical for formal or business interactions. In France, a light kiss on each cheek is also customary in informal settings. In Greece, a handshake is common, while in Turkey, it is polite to greet with a handshake, particularly in formal situations. Respect local customs and follow the lead of locals when it comes to greetings.

- Cultural Sensitivities: Respect local customs and dress codes, especially when visiting religious sites. In many Mediterranean countries, modest clothing is required for entering churches or mosques. Be mindful of local attitudes and behaviors, and always approach interactions with a sense of respect and openness.

By understanding these aspects of currency, language, and etiquette, you'll be better equipped to navigate Mediterranean ports and enjoy your travels with confidence and ease.

CHAPTER 4
WESTERN MEDITERRANEAN PORTS

Exploring the Western Mediterranean ports opens a world of vibrant culture, historic sites, and stunning coastlines. This region, a crossroads of history and modernity, offers a rich tapestry of experiences that are sure to captivate any traveler. From the sun-drenched shores of Spain and France to the enchanting Italian Riviera, the Western Mediterranean is a treasure trove of unique destinations waiting to be discovered.

Barcelona, Spain

Barcelona, Spain, is a vibrant Mediterranean city brimming with charm and history, making it an irresistible stop on any Mediterranean cruise. With its lively streets, stunning architecture, and rich cultural heritage, Barcelona offers something for every traveler. Here's a guide to help you make the most of your visit to this captivating city.

Start your exploration in the heart of Barcelona with a visit to La Rambla, the city's bustling main street. Here, you'll find a lively promenade filled with shops, street performers, and cafes. A stroll down La Rambla is a great way to soak in the local atmosphere. Don't miss the famous La Boqueria Market along the way, where you can sample fresh produce, meats, and local delicacies.

No visit to Barcelona is complete without experiencing the architectural marvels of Antoni Gaudí. Begin with the

Sagrada Familia, Gaudí's iconic basilica that has been under construction since 1882. Its intricate facades and towering spires are a testament to Gaudí's genius. Be sure to book tickets in advance to avoid long lines.

Next, head to Park Güell, another Gaudí masterpiece. This colorful park offers stunning views of the city and is adorned with whimsical mosaics and sculptures. The park's unique design and beautiful gardens make it a perfect spot for a leisurely walk.

Explore the Gothic Quarter, a maze of narrow medieval streets that reveal Barcelona's past. Wander through Plaça Reial, a lively square surrounded by elegant arcades and palm trees. Visit the Barcelona Cathedral in the Gothic Quarter, a grand example of Catalan Gothic architecture with its impressive facade and peaceful cloister.

For art enthusiasts, the Picasso Museum is a must-visit. Located in the Gothic Quarter, it houses an extensive collection of works by Pablo Picasso, showcasing his evolution as an artist. The museum is set in a series of medieval mansions, adding to its charm.

When it comes to outdoor activities, Barceloneta Beach is a great place to relax. Located near the old fishing district, it offers a sandy stretch where you can sunbathe, swim, or enjoy a meal at one of the beachfront restaurants. For a more scenic experience, take a leisurely walk or bike ride along the Barcelona Waterfront, which extends from Barceloneta to Port Olímpic.

Montjuïc Hill provides panoramic views of the city and a range of attractions. You can visit the Montjuïc Castle, take a cable car ride, or explore the Magic Fountain that hosts evening light and music shows. The hill is also home to the National Art Museum of Catalonia (MNAC), which features an impressive collection of Catalan art.

For dining, Barcelona offers a wealth of culinary delights. Try Tapas 24 for a range of delicious tapas in a casual setting. El Quim de la Boqueria in La Boqueria Market is known for its fresh, vibrant dishes. For a fine dining experience, Cinc Sentits provides a modern twist on Catalan cuisine, earning it a Michelin star.

In terms of accommodation, Barcelona caters to various budgets. Hotel 1898 on La Rambla offers a blend of luxury and historical charm with its elegant rooms and rooftop pool. For a mid-range option, Hotel Casa Fuster combines classic architecture with modern comforts and is well-located for exploring the city. Budget travelers might opt for Hostel Generator, which provides clean, affordable lodging with a trendy atmosphere.

Barcelona's Mediterranean allure makes it an enchanting destination. From its artistic heritage to its lively street life and beautiful beaches, Barcelona offers a memorable experience for every traveler.

Marseille, France

Marseille, France, stands as a dynamic gateway to the Western Mediterranean, blending rich history, cultural vibrancy, and stunning coastal beauty. As France's second-largest city and a historic port, Marseille offers a unique blend of old-world charm and contemporary allure. Here's a guide to help you uncover the best this captivating city has to offer.

Start your visit at the Vieux-Port, the historic Old Port of Marseille, which has been the city's heart for centuries. The bustling harbor is lined with charming cafés and restaurants where you can sit and watch the lively activity of fishing boats and yachts. It's also a great spot to soak in the local atmosphere and enjoy some people-watching.

No visit to Marseille is complete without seeing the Basilique Notre-Dame de la Garde. This stunning basilica, perched on a hilltop overlooking the city, offers panoramic views of Marseille and the Mediterranean Sea. The basilica itself is a masterpiece of 19th-century architecture, adorned with intricate mosaics and a towering statue of the Virgin Mary. A visit here is not only a spiritual experience but also an opportunity to capture breathtaking photos of the cityscape.

Explore the historic district of Le Panier, Marseille's oldest neighborhood, known for its narrow, winding streets and colorful façades. This area is a haven for art lovers and craft enthusiasts, with numerous galleries, boutiques, and street art. The vibrant atmosphere and charming squares make it a perfect place to wander and discover local treasures.

For a taste of Marseille's maritime history, visit the Musée des Civilisations de l'Europe et de la Méditerranée (MuCEM). This modern museum, located on the waterfront, explores Mediterranean cultures and history through interactive exhibits and stunning architecture. The museum's design, with its latticework facade, is as impressive as the collections inside. Adjacent to the museum is the Fort Saint-Jean, which offers great views of the harbor and the city.

Outdoor enthusiasts will enjoy the Calanques National Park, a beautiful stretch of rugged coastline and turquoise waters just a short drive from the city. The park is perfect for hiking, swimming, and taking in the dramatic cliffs and serene coves. You can explore the park on foot, or take a boat tour to appreciate its natural beauty from the water.

For dining, Marseille boasts a range of excellent options. Try Chez Fonfon, a local favorite known for its traditional Bouillabaisse, a classic Provençal fish stew. For a more casual experience, visit Le Relais 50, which offers a variety of Mediterranean dishes in a relaxed setting. If you're in the mood for something more refined, La Table de l'Olivier offers modern French cuisine with an emphasis on fresh, local ingredients.

In terms of accommodation, Marseille offers options to suit various budgets. For a touch of luxury, consider the InterContinental Marseille - Hotel Dieu, located near the

Old Port with elegant rooms and stunning views. If you're looking for something more mid-range, the Hôtel Edmond Rostand offers comfortable accommodations in a central location, ideal for exploring the city. Budget travelers might opt for the Hotel Ibis Marseille, which provides basic yet comfortable lodging with easy access to the city's attractions.

Marseille's rich tapestry of history, culture, and natural beauty ensures that visitors will find plenty to explore and enjoy. From its historic port and grand basilica to its vibrant neighborhoods and stunning coastal landscapes, Marseille promises a memorable Mediterranean experience.

Nice, France

Nice, France, is a sparkling gem on the French Riviera, renowned for its stunning coastal beauty and vibrant cultural scene. As a popular port on Mediterranean cruises, Nice offers a delightful blend of picturesque landscapes, historical charm, and sophisticated allure. Here's a guide to help you fully enjoy your time in this captivating city.

Begin your visit with a stroll along the Promenade des Anglais, Nice's iconic waterfront boulevard. Stretching for several kilometers along the azure Mediterranean Sea, this scenic walkway is perfect for a leisurely walk or a bike ride. Along the promenade, you'll find a mix of historic hotels, charming cafés, and public beaches. It's also a great spot to enjoy a sunset or simply take in the fresh sea breeze.

Head to the Old Town, or Vieux Nice, where you can get lost in a labyrinth of narrow streets lined with colorful buildings, bustling markets, and quaint shops. The Cours Saleya, a vibrant market square in the heart of Old Town, is a must-visit. Here, you can explore the flower and food markets, which offer a range of local produce, cheeses, and artisan goods. The lively atmosphere and array of street vendors make this a great place for both shopping and sampling local delicacies.

Make sure to visit the Promenade du Paillon, a lush park that offers a refreshing green space in the city. The park features a mix of fountains, playgrounds, and open spaces perfect for relaxing or enjoying a picnic. It's an excellent spot to escape the hustle and bustle and enjoy some tranquility.

No trip to Nice is complete without experiencing its rich cultural heritage. Visit the Musée Matisse, located in the Cimiez neighborhood, to see a substantial collection of works by the famed artist Henri Matisse. The museum is housed in a beautiful villa surrounded by gardens, enhancing the overall experience. Another cultural highlight is the Musée d'Art Moderne et d'Art Contemporain, which features a diverse collection of modern and contemporary art.

For outdoor enthusiasts, the Colline du Château (Castle Hill) offers breathtaking panoramic views of Nice and the surrounding coastline. Although the castle itself is in ruins, the hill provides some of the best vantage points in the city. You can either hike up or take the elevator to reach the top and enjoy the expansive views.

When it comes to dining, Nice is known for its excellent cuisine. For a taste of traditional Niçoise dishes, head to La Merenda, a cozy restaurant known for its authentic local fare. Try specialties like socca (chickpea pancake) and salade Niçoise. For a more upscale dining experience, Le Chantecler, located in the Negresco Hotel, offers a refined menu of French cuisine with a focus on fresh, local ingredients. For a casual yet delightful meal, visit Chez Pipo, famous for its delicious socca and other local specialties.

In terms of accommodation, Nice offers a range of options to suit various budgets. For a luxurious stay, consider the iconic Hotel Negresco, a historic palace hotel located right on the Promenade des Anglais with elegant rooms and top-notch amenities. If you prefer something more mid-range, the Hôtel La Pérouse offers comfortable accommodations with stunning sea views and is conveniently located near the Old Town. Budget travelers will find good value at Hotel Rossetti, which is centrally located and offers cozy rooms without breaking the bank.

Nice's blend of stunning scenery, rich cultural experiences, and excellent dining makes it a must-visit destination on the Mediterranean coast. Whether you're strolling along the promenade, exploring historic neighborhoods, or savoring local cuisine, Nice promises an unforgettable experience.

Monaco

Monaco, a tiny but dazzling gem nestled on the French Riviera, is renowned for its opulence, glamour, and stunning Mediterranean vistas. As a port of call on a Western Mediterranean cruise, Monaco offers a wealth of experiences that blend luxury with rich cultural heritage. Here's a detailed guide to help you explore this captivating destination.

Start your Monaco adventure with a visit to the Monte Carlo Casino, a symbol of the city-state's lavish lifestyle. Even if you're not a gambler, the casino's grand architecture and luxurious interiors are worth admiring. Designed by architect Charles Garnier, the building boasts ornate decorations and stunning frescoes. Consider taking a guided tour to fully appreciate the opulence and learn about its history.

From the casino, it's a short walk to Casino Square, where you'll find high-end shops, elegant cafes, and the iconic Hotel de Paris. This square is a prime spot for people-watching and soaking in the luxurious atmosphere of Monaco.

Next, explore the Prince's Palace of Monaco, perched atop a rocky promontory overlooking the harbor. This historic palace is the residence of the Grimaldi family. Watch the Changing of the Guard ceremony, which takes place daily at 11:55 a.m., and tour the state apartments to see the opulent rooms and royal collections.

Head to the Monaco Cathedral, located in the old town of Monaco-Ville. This serene Romanesque church is the final resting place of several members of the Grimaldi family, including Princess Grace. The cathedral's elegant simplicity and tranquil atmosphere provide a peaceful retreat from the city's bustle.

For a taste of Monaco's natural beauty, visit the Jardin Exotique (Exotic Garden). This stunning garden features a diverse collection of succulents and cacti from around the world, set against dramatic cliffside views of the Mediterranean. The garden also includes a cave and a lookout point that offers panoramic views of Monaco and beyond.

Another great outdoor spot is Monaco Harbor, where you can enjoy a leisurely stroll along the quays, marvel at the luxury yachts, and take in the spectacular waterfront views. The harbor is a fantastic place to relax and enjoy the vibrant maritime atmosphere.

Culturally, Monaco offers a rich tapestry of experiences. The Oceanographic Museum is a must-see, showcasing marine life and oceanographic research. Perched on a cliff, the museum houses impressive exhibits and an aquarium, making it a fascinating stop for all ages.

When it comes to dining, Monaco has an array of options to suit various tastes and budgets. For a taste of Monaco's luxury, dine at Le Louis XV – Alain Ducasse, located in the Hotel de Paris. This Michelin-starred restaurant offers exquisite French cuisine in an opulent setting. For a more casual yet refined experience, try Café de Paris

Monte-Carlo, which offers a mix of classic French dishes and stunning views of Casino Square. If you're looking for something more affordable, Le Café de Paris is a good choice for casual meals with a great atmosphere.

Accommodation in Monaco ranges from the ultra-luxurious to more modest options. For a truly extravagant experience, stay at the Hotel Negresco, which offers world-class amenities and is located close to Casino Square. If you prefer a mid-range option, the Columbus Monte-Carlo provides comfortable accommodations with a chic, modern design. For budget-conscious travelers, the Hotel Ambassador Monaco offers a good balance of comfort and affordability, situated a short distance from the main attractions.

Monaco's blend of luxury, history, and natural beauty makes it a captivating destination on the Mediterranean cruise route. Whether you're exploring grand casinos, admiring royal palaces, or enjoying serene gardens, Monaco promises an unforgettable experience filled with elegance and charm.

Livorno (Florence/Pisa), Italy

Livorno, a charming Italian port city on the Tuscan coast, serves as a gateway to some of Italy's most renowned destinations, including Florence and Pisa. Known for its historic canals, vibrant markets, and strategic location, Livorno is a delightful stop on any Western Mediterranean cruise. Here's a comprehensive guide to help you make the most of your visit.

Start your exploration with a visit to the historic canals of Livorno. These canals, often compared to Venice's, are a remnant of the city's 17th-century development. You can take a leisurely stroll along the canals or enjoy a gondola ride, which offers a unique perspective of the city's architecture and charming bridges.

The Terrazza Mascagni is another must-see. This scenic promenade along the waterfront features a stunning checkerboard-patterned pavement and offers breathtaking views of the Tyrrhenian Sea. It's a perfect spot for a relaxing walk or a sunset photo opportunity.

For a taste of Livorno's local flavor, explore the Mercato Centrale. This bustling market, housed in a beautiful building with an iron and glass facade, is filled with fresh produce, local cheeses, meats, and pastries. It's a great place to sample Italian specialties and soak up the lively atmosphere.

If you're keen on venturing further, Livorno's location provides easy access to two iconic Italian cities: Florence and Pisa. Florence, with its Renaissance splendor, is just about an hour's drive away. The city is renowned for its art and architecture, with top attractions including the Uffizi Gallery, home to masterpieces by Botticelli and Michelangelo, and the Florence Cathedral, known for its magnificent dome designed by Brunelleschi.

Pisa, about a 30-minute drive from Livorno, is famous for the Leaning Tower of Pisa. This architectural marvel is part of the larger Piazza dei Miracoli, which also includes the Pisa Cathedral and Baptistery. Climbing the Leaning Tower is a unique experience, offering panoramic views of the surrounding area.

In Livorno, you can enjoy various outdoor activities. For a relaxing day, head to Calafuria Beach, located a short drive from the city center. This picturesque beach features clear waters and rocky cliffs, ideal for swimming and sunbathing. Alternatively, explore the Livorno Promenade, where you can walk or bike along the seafront and enjoy the scenic views.

Culturally, Livorno has much to offer. Visit the Museo Civico Giovanni Fattori, which showcases works by the 19th-century artist Giovanni Fattori and other Italian painters. The museum is located in a beautiful historic building and offers insight into Livorno's artistic heritage.

Dining in Livorno is a treat for the senses. For a traditional Italian meal, try Trattoria da Galileo, known for its seafood dishes and local specialties. If you're in the mood for pizza, Pizzeria La Pizzaccia offers delicious, thin-crust pizzas with a variety of toppings. For a more upscale experience, Ristorante Venezia provides elegant dining with a menu featuring fresh local ingredients and classic Italian flavors.

When it comes to accommodation, Livorno offers options for various budgets. For a luxurious stay, consider the Grand Hotel Palazzo Livorno, which features elegant rooms and a prime location overlooking the sea. If you're looking for a mid-range option, the Hotel Gran Duca offers comfortable accommodations in the city center, close to major attractions. Budget travelers might find the Hotel Citta a good choice, providing simple, clean rooms and convenient access to the port and city center.

Livorno's blend of historical charm, access to Florence and Pisa, and beautiful coastal scenery makes it a fantastic destination on your Mediterranean cruise. Whether you're exploring the canals, indulging in local cuisine, or venturing to nearby cities, Livorno promises a memorable and enriching experience.

Civitavecchia (Rome), Italy

Civitavecchia, Italy, serves as the primary gateway to Rome, one of the world's most iconic cities. As a cruise port on the Western Mediterranean route, Civitavecchia offers a convenient starting point for exploring the rich history, culture, and attractions of Rome. Here's a comprehensive guide to help you make the most of your visit.

Begin your journey by taking advantage of Civitavecchia's proximity to Rome, which is about an hour's drive away. The city's bustling port area provides easy access to transportation options like trains and shuttle services, making the trip to Rome straightforward and efficient.

Once in Rome, immerse yourself in the city's vast historical and cultural heritage. Start with the Colosseum, an ancient amphitheater and one of the most recognizable symbols of Rome. This monumental structure offers a glimpse into the grandeur of Roman engineering and gladiatorial combat. To avoid long lines, it's advisable to book tickets in advance or consider a guided tour.

From the Colosseum, walk to the nearby Roman Forum. This sprawling archaeological site was once the heart of ancient Rome and is filled with ruins of temples, basilicas, and public spaces. Wandering through the Forum, you'll feel as if you've stepped back in time.

A short walk from the Forum will lead you to the Pantheon, a remarkably well-preserved ancient temple. Its massive dome and oculus are architectural marvels, and the building's interior, now a church, is equally impressive.

No visit to Rome is complete without exploring the Vatican City. The Vatican Museums house an extraordinary collection of art and historical artifacts, including Michelangelo's frescoes in the Sistine Chapel. The adjacent St. Peter's Basilica is another must-see, renowned for its stunning dome designed by Michelangelo and its grand interior.

For outdoor activities, stroll through Villa Borghese, Rome's central park. This expansive green space offers gardens, lakes, and museums, including the Galleria Borghese, which features a superb collection of art, including works by Caravaggio and Bernini. Renting a bike or rowing a boat on the park's lake are enjoyable ways to explore the area.

Take a leisurely walk through Trastevere, one of Rome's most charming neighborhoods. With its narrow, winding streets, vibrant atmosphere, and beautiful piazzas, Trastevere is perfect for a relaxed exploration. The Santa Maria in Trastevere church, with its stunning mosaics, is a highlight in this area.

When it comes to dining, Rome offers an array of delicious options. For authentic Italian cuisine, try Da Enzo al 29, a small trattoria known for its traditional Roman dishes like carbonara and cacio e pepe. For pizza, head to Pizzarium, which offers a variety of creative toppings on deliciously crispy crusts. For a more upscale dining experience, La Pergola, a Michelin-starred restaurant, provides exquisite dishes and panoramic views of the city.

In terms of accommodation, Rome has options for every budget. For a luxurious stay, consider Hotel Hassler, located near the Spanish Steps and offering opulent rooms and exceptional service. Hotel Artemide, in a central location, provides a blend of comfort and modern amenities, making it a great mid-range choice. For budget travelers, Hotel Delle Province offers clean, comfortable rooms at an affordable rate and is well-connected to public transport.

Civitavecchia, with its easy access to Rome, provides a gateway to exploring one of the world's most historically and culturally significant cities. Whether you're marveling at ancient ruins, savoring authentic Italian cuisine, or simply enjoying the vibrant atmosphere, your visit promises to be a memorable experience.

Naples, Italy

Naples, Italy, is a vibrant city brimming with history, culture, and gastronomic delights. Nestled on the western coast of Italy, this bustling port city is a gateway to some of the most iconic attractions in the region. As a cruise port on the Western Mediterranean route, Naples offers a rich tapestry of experiences that blend ancient history with lively street life. Here's a detailed guide to help you explore this fascinating city.

Start your Naples adventure with a visit to the Naples National Archaeological Museum. This world-renowned museum houses one of the most extensive collections of Greco-Roman antiquities. Highlights include artifacts from Pompeii and Herculaneum, such as intricate mosaics, statues, and everyday objects that offer a glimpse into ancient life.

From the museum, take a short walk to the Historic Centre of Naples, a UNESCO World Heritage site. Here, narrow streets are lined with historical buildings and vibrant markets. The Spaccanapoli street, which slices through the heart of the old town, is a lively area filled with artisan shops, cafes, and traditional pizzerias. This is also where you'll find the Naples Cathedral, known for its stunning Gothic and Baroque architecture.

A must-see in Naples is the Royal Palace of Naples. Situated on Piazza del Plebiscito, this grand palace offers a glimpse into the opulent lifestyle of the Neapolitan royalty. The palace's lavish rooms and historic artifacts are complemented by beautiful views of the surrounding area from the palace grounds.

For outdoor enthusiasts, the Vesuvius Volcano is an exciting excursion. Just a short drive from Naples, this active volcano provides an opportunity to hike up to the crater and enjoy panoramic views of the Bay of Naples and the surrounding landscape. If you're interested in history, the nearby Pompeii and Herculaneum archaeological sites are not to be missed. These ancient cities were buried under volcanic ash in AD 79 and have been remarkably well-preserved.

Another great outdoor spot is the Naples Waterfront. Take a leisurely stroll along the Lungomare promenade, which offers stunning views of the Bay of Naples and the majestic Mount Vesuvius. The area is also home to Castel dell'Ovo, a medieval fortress that provides excellent photo opportunities and insight into Naples' maritime history.

Culturally, Naples is rich with experiences. Visit the Teatro di San Carlo, Italy's oldest opera house, to catch a performance or take a guided tour of this historic venue.

The Sansevero Chapel, famous for its extraordinary sculpture of the Veiled Christ, is another cultural highlight. Its intricate marble work and religious art offer a profound and moving experience.

When it comes to dining, Naples is the birthplace of pizza, and there's no better place to enjoy a classic Neapolitan pizza. L'Antica Pizzeria da Michele is a legendary spot, renowned for its simple yet delicious pizzas. For a more refined dining experience, Palazzo Petrucci offers gourmet Italian cuisine with a focus on fresh, local ingredients and stunning views of the bay. If you're in the mood for something different, Trattoria da Nennella offers hearty local dishes in a lively, casual setting.

Accommodation in Naples caters to various budgets. For a luxurious stay, Grand Hotel Vesuvio offers elegant rooms with stunning views of the Bay of Naples and exceptional service. Hotel Piazza Bellini is a great mid-range option, located in the heart of the historic center and known for its stylish decor and convenient location. Budget travelers might consider Hotel Europeo, which provides clean, comfortable accommodations in a central location without breaking the bank.

Naples, with its blend of historic charm, cultural richness, and culinary excellence, provides a memorable experience for visitors. Whether you're exploring ancient ruins, savoring world-famous pizza, or strolling along picturesque waterfronts, Naples offers a captivating glimpse into the heart of Italy.

Palermo, Italy

Palermo, the vibrant capital of Sicily, is a city rich with history, culture, and culinary delights. As a prominent port city in the Western Mediterranean, Palermo offers a range of experiences that reflect its diverse heritage and lively atmosphere. Whether you're wandering through bustling markets or discovering historic landmarks, Palermo promises an unforgettable adventure.

Start your visit at the Palermo Cathedral, an architectural marvel that showcases a blend of Norman, Gothic, and Baroque styles. The cathedral's intricate façade and stunning interior also house the royal tombs of the Norman kings. For breathtaking views of the city and its surroundings, climb to the rooftop.

A short walk from the cathedral leads you to Quattro Canti, an iconic Baroque square at the heart of Palermo. This octagonal piazza, adorned with ornate statues and fountains, offers a perfect vantage point to appreciate the city's architectural splendor and vibrant street life.

Delve into Palermo's history with a visit to the Palazzo dei Normanni (Norman Palace). Once the seat of the Kings of Sicily, this historic building now hosts the Sicilian Regional Assembly. The Palatine Chapel within the palace is renowned for its stunning Arab-Norman mosaics and intricate wooden ceilings.

Another must-see is the Teatro Massimo, one of Italy's largest and most prestigious opera houses. The theatre's opulent interiors and impressive performances make it a cultural gem. A guided tour of the theatre provides insight into its grandeur and history.

For outdoor enthusiasts, Palermo offers several charming spots. The Orto Botanico (Botanical Garden) is a peaceful retreat with a diverse collection of plants from around the world. Stroll through its lush pathways and enjoy a moment of tranquility away from the city's hustle.

The Palermo Waterfront is another delightful area to explore. A leisurely stroll along the seafront promenade offers stunning views of the Mediterranean Sea and an opportunity to relax in nearby parks. The Foro Italico, a large green space along the waterfront, is ideal for a leisurely walk or a picnic.

Culturally, Palermo is a treasure trove. Explore the Capuchin Catacombs, an eerie yet fascinating site where mummified remains are displayed in various states of preservation. This unique attraction provides insight into historical burial practices and the city's past.

Palermo is also renowned for its street food and vibrant culinary scene. Sample local favorites like arancini (stuffed rice balls) and pane con la milza (spleen sandwich) from street vendors. For a sit-down meal, Antica Focacceria San Francesco offers traditional Sicilian dishes in a historic setting. For a more upscale dining experience, Osteria Ballarò serves refined Sicilian cuisine with a focus on fresh, local ingredients.

Accommodation in Palermo caters to various budgets. For a luxurious stay, the Grand Hotel Piazza Borsa offers elegant rooms and excellent amenities in a prime location. Hotel Porta Felice is a stylish mid-range option known for its comfortable rooms and central position. Budget travelers will appreciate Hotel Vecchio Borgo, which provides clean and affordable accommodations close to the city center.

With its rich history, vibrant culture, and delicious cuisine, Palermo offers an enriching experience for every visitor. Whether exploring historic sites, savoring local delicacies, or relaxing along the waterfront, Palermo provides a captivating journey into the heart of Sicily.

Valletta, Malta

Valletta, the fortified capital of Malta, is a gem of the Western Mediterranean, offering a rich blend of history, culture, and scenic beauty. As a prominent cruise port, Valletta invites visitors to explore its compact yet vibrant streets, brimming with Baroque architecture, historic landmarks, and delightful Mediterranean charm.

Start your journey at the Upper Barracca Gardens, which provide stunning panoramic views of the Grand Harbour. This tranquil spot is perfect for a leisurely stroll among beautifully manicured gardens and offers a peaceful respite from the city's bustling streets.

A short walk from the gardens brings you to St. John's Co-Cathedral, one of Valletta's most impressive landmarks. This 16th-century cathedral, with its opulent Baroque interior and intricate Caravaggio paintings, is a masterpiece of ecclesiastical art. The cathedral's floor, adorned with elaborate tombstones, adds to the grandeur of the experience.

Explore the Grand Master's Palace, a historic building that once served as the residence of the Grand Masters of the Knights of St. John. Today, it houses the Malta Parliament and features an impressive collection of armor and period furnishings. The palace's State Rooms are particularly noteworthy for their ornate décor.

For a taste of Valletta's history, visit the National Museum of Archaeology, which houses artifacts from Malta's prehistoric period. Highlights include ancient pottery, jewelry, and statues that offer a glimpse into the island's early civilizations.

To enjoy the city's outdoor spaces, head to Lower Barracca Gardens. These serene gardens are located near the port and offer a relaxing spot with beautiful views over the harbor and the surrounding forts. It's a great place to unwind and soak in the local atmosphere.

Valletta's vibrant street life and bustling markets can be explored at the Valletta Market, also known as Is-Suq tal-Belt. This recently renovated market is a lively hub where you can find fresh local produce, gourmet foods, and artisan products.

Culturally, Valletta is rich with experiences. The Malta Experience is an engaging multimedia presentation that provides a comprehensive overview of Malta's history. It's an excellent introduction for first-time visitors. Additionally, the Teatru Manoel, Malta's oldest theatre, offers a variety of performances and tours showcasing its historic and architectural significance.

When it comes to dining, Valletta offers a range of options. For a taste of local cuisine, visit Nenu the Artisan Baker, known for its traditional Maltese dishes like rabbit stew and ftira (Maltese bread). Rampila, located within the historic city walls, provides a refined dining experience with a menu that blends Mediterranean flavors with contemporary flair. For a more casual meal, Caffe Cordina is a charming spot for coffee and pastries in a historic setting.

Accommodation in Valletta ranges from luxurious to budget-friendly options. Hotel Phoenicia Malta is a top choice for a luxurious stay, offering elegant rooms, a beautiful pool, and exceptional service. Hotel Palazzo Prince d'Orange provides a stylish mid-range option with comfortable accommodations and a central location. For budget travelers, Castille Hotel offers clean and simple rooms with a prime location close to the city's main attractions.

Valletta, with its rich history, stunning architecture, and vibrant culture, provides a captivating experience for every visitor. Whether you're exploring historic sites, enjoying scenic views, or savoring local cuisine, Valletta promises a memorable journey into the heart of Malta.

CHAPTER 5
ICONIC PORTS OF THE EASTERN MEDITERRANEAN

The Eastern Mediterranean is a region of unparalleled allure, where ancient histories, diverse cultures, and breathtaking landscapes converge to offer a travel experience like no other. This chapter will guide you through some of the most captivating ports in this area, each one a gateway to its unique blend of heritage and natural beauty.

Imagine a journey that takes you from the sun-drenched shores of Greece to the historic cities of Turkey, and then to the rich tapestries of Cyprus. The Eastern Mediterranean ports are renowned for their vibrant local life, stunning architecture, and rich historical tapestry. Each destination provides a unique entry point into the soul of its country, offering travelers the chance to immerse themselves in a blend of past and present.

As you explore the Eastern Mediterranean, you'll discover cities that are steeped in myth and legend. From the storied ruins of ancient civilizations to the lively markets and serene coastlines, the region unfolds a rich narrative that has captivated explorers, historians, and travelers for centuries.

The crystal-clear waters of the Aegean and Mediterranean seas frame this region, creating a stunning backdrop for its historical and cultural treasures. The sun-bathed landscapes are dotted with charming villages, majestic ruins, and vibrant urban centers. Here, you'll encounter a mosaic of cultures that have mingled and evolved over millennia, each leaving its mark on the region's distinctive character.

In the Eastern Mediterranean, history and modernity walk hand in hand. You'll find ancient ruins that tell tales of bygone eras, juxtaposed with bustling markets where contemporary life thrives. Whether you're wandering through the labyrinthine streets of an ancient city or relaxing by a pristine beach, the contrasts and harmonies of the Eastern Mediterranean create a unique travel experience.

This journey through the Eastern Mediterranean offers more than just sightseeing. It's an invitation to dive into the region's diverse cuisines, where aromatic spices and fresh ingredients combine to create culinary masterpieces. It's an opportunity to engage with local traditions, from traditional festivals to artisanal crafts, providing a deeper understanding of the vibrant cultures that define this part of the world.

As you traverse these ports, you'll encounter a variety of landscapes and cityscapes, each with its own story to tell. The ancient temples, medieval fortresses, and sprawling bazaars are not just remnants of the past; they are living parts of the present-day experience. The warm hospitality of the locals, the rich flavors of the food, and the stunning natural beauty all contribute to a journey that is both enriching and unforgettable. The Eastern Mediterranean ports offer a gateway to an enchanting realm where history and modern life blend seamlessly, and where every corner holds the promise of discovery and wonder.

Athens (Piraeus), Greece

Athens, the capital of Greece, stands as a living testament to the grandeur of ancient civilization and the vibrancy of modern life. As the primary cruise port of Piraeus, Athens welcomes travelers with its rich tapestry of history, culture, and energetic street life. This guide will navigate you through the must-see attractions and experiences in this historic city.

Start your exploration at the Acropolis of Athens, the crowning jewel of ancient Greece. This ancient citadel, perched atop a rocky outcrop, is home to some of the most iconic structures of classical architecture, including the Parthenon, the Erechtheion, and the Temple of Athena Nike. The Parthenon, with its grand columns and intricate sculptures, embodies the zenith of ancient Greek artistry and religious devotion. A stroll around the 9Acropolis offers not only a glimpse into ancient 44324(history but also breathtaking views of the city below.

From the Acropolis, make your way to the Acropolis Museum, an architectural marvel itself. This modern museum houses a vast collection of artifacts from the Acropolis site, including sculptures, pottery, and friezes. The museum's glass floors provide a fascinating view of the excavations below, enhancing the experience of exploring Greece's ancient past.

A visit to Plaka, the charming old neighborhood of Athens, is a must. Wander through its narrow, winding streets lined with neoclassical houses, quaint shops, and traditional tavernas. The area's lively atmosphere and historical architecture create a picturesque setting for leisurely exploration. Don't miss the opportunity to visit the Roman Agora and the Tower of the Winds, ancient structures that reflect Athens' rich history of commerce and public life.

For a taste of Athenian outdoor life, head to the National Garden of Athens, a serene escape in the heart of the city. This lush green space offers shaded pathways, tranquil ponds, and a small zoo, providing a peaceful respite from the urban bustle. Nearby, the Zappeion Hall and the Panathenaic Stadium, the site of the first modern Olympic Games, are worth a visit for their historical significance and stunning architecture.

Athens is also known for its vibrant street life and markets. The Monastiraki Flea Market is a bustling hub where you can find everything from antiques and souvenirs to local crafts and fresh produce. The adjacent Athens Central Market offers a sensory overload of colors, sounds, and aromas, with vendors selling a variety of meats, fish, and spices.

When it comes to dining, Athens offers a delightful array of options. For traditional Greek cuisine, visit Tzitzikas kai Mermigas, a popular spot known for its modern takes on classic dishes like moussaka and souvlaki. Kuzina offers a more contemporary dining experience with a menu that blends traditional Greek flavors with innovative touches. For a relaxed, casual meal, Kostas is famed for its delicious souvlaki and friendly atmosphere.

Accommodation in Athens caters to all tastes and budgets. For a luxurious stay, King George Hotel offers elegant rooms and impeccable service with stunning views of the Acropolis. Electra Metropolis is a stylish mid-range option featuring modern amenities and a rooftop bar with panoramic views of the city. Budget travelers will find comfort at Hotel Attalos, which provides clean, affordable rooms and a convenient location near Monastiraki Square.

Athens, with its rich historical heritage, vibrant street life, and diverse culinary scene, offers an enriching and engaging experience for travelers. From exploring ancient ruins to enjoying modern Greek cuisine, this dynamic city provides a memorable introduction to the heart of Greece.

Mykonos, Greece

Mykonos, a dazzling gem in the Aegean Sea, is renowned for its stunning beaches, vibrant nightlife, and charming Cycladic architecture. As a premier cruise port in the Eastern Mediterranean, Mykonos offers a delightful mix of relaxation, exploration, and cultural experiences, making it a must-visit destination for travelers.

Mykonos Town, often referred to as Chora. This picturesque town is a labyrinth of narrow, winding streets lined with whitewashed buildings adorned with colorful bougainvillea. The iconic windmills perched on a hill offer panoramic views of the town and the sea. Nearby, the charming Little Venice district is perfect for a leisurely stroll along the waterfront, where you can enjoy the sunset and admire the historic buildings that seem to spill into the sea.

One of the top attractions is the Church of Panagia Paraportiani, a stunning architectural marvel with its distinctive whitewashed domes. Located in the heart of Mykonos Town, this church is one of the most photographed landmarks on the island and offers a glimpse into the island's religious heritage.

For those interested in history, the Archaeological Museum of Mykonos houses artifacts from the ancient Greek civilization, including pottery and sculptures from nearby Delos Island, which is a significant archaeological site in its own right. A day trip to Delos, accessible by ferry, is highly recommended. This uninhabited island is an open-air museum, home to extensive ruins including temples, statues, and ancient homes, and provides a fascinating insight into ancient Greek culture.

Outdoor enthusiasts will find plenty to enjoy on Mykonos. The island boasts several beautiful beaches, each with its unique charm. Psarou Beach is known for its crystal-clear waters and upscale vibe, attracting a chic crowd. Paradise Beach and Super Paradise Beach are famous for their lively atmosphere and beach parties, offering a perfect blend of sun, sea, and music. For a quieter experience, head to Elia Beach or Agios Sostis Beach, where you can relax in a more serene setting.

A visit to Mykonos isn't complete without experiencing its vibrant dining scene. For a taste of traditional Greek cuisine, try Kiki's Tavern, an open-air restaurant near Agios Sostis Beach, known for its delicious grilled meats and fresh salads. For a more upscale dining experience, Nobu Mykonos offers a sophisticated setting with renowned Japanese-Peruvian dishes and stunning views of the Aegean. For a casual meal with a view, head to the popular seaside restaurant, M-eating, which offers a range of Mediterranean dishes in a relaxed atmosphere.

Accommodation on Mykonos caters to various preferences and budgets. For luxury, the Santa Marina, a Luxury Collection Resort, offers elegant rooms, private beach access, and exceptional service. The Mykonos Blu Grecotel Exclusive Resort is another top choice, featuring stunning views, a private beach, and high-end amenities. For a more budget-friendly option, the Hotel Petasos Beach is conveniently located and offers comfortable accommodations with easy access to the beach and town.

Mykonos, with its blend of beautiful landscapes, rich cultural heritage, and lively atmosphere, promises an unforgettable experience. Whether you're exploring historical sites, relaxing on sandy shores, or savoring exquisite local cuisine, this vibrant island invites you to immerse yourself in its unique charm and energy.

Santorini, Greece

Santorini, an enchanting island in the Aegean Sea, is a highlight of the Eastern Mediterranean cruise circuit. Famous for its dramatic volcanic landscapes, iconic white-washed buildings with blue domes, and stunning sunsets, Santorini offers a unique blend of natural beauty, rich history, and vibrant local culture.

Start your exploration in Fira, the island's bustling capital. Perched on the edge of the caldera, Fira provides breathtaking panoramic views of the turquoise sea and the surrounding volcanic islands. Wander through its narrow streets lined with boutique shops, art galleries, and charming cafes. The vibrant atmosphere makes it a perfect place for leisurely strolling and people-watching.

From Fira, make your way to Oia, one of the most picturesque villages on the island. Oia is renowned for its stunning sunsets, which are best enjoyed from one of the many terraces or cafes overlooking the caldera. The village is a maze of white-washed buildings with blue-domed churches and narrow alleys adorned with boutique shops and art galleries. It's a romantic setting ideal for exploring and capturing unforgettable photographs.

For those interested in history, a visit to the ancient site of Akrotiri is a must. This well-preserved Minoan city was buried under volcanic ash during the eruption of 1627 BC and provides a fascinating glimpse into ancient life on Santorini. Walk through the ruins and explore the remains of buildings, frescoes, and artifacts that reveal the sophistication of this early civilization.

Outdoor enthusiasts will appreciate the island's natural beauty. Santorini's volcanic landscape offers unique experiences such as hiking the trail from Fira to Oia, which takes you along the caldera's edge with spectacular views. Another popular destination is the Red Beach, known for its striking red volcanic sand and clear waters, perfect for swimming and sunbathing. For a more serene beach experience, visit Kamari Beach or Perissa Beach, which offer black sand and are equipped with facilities for a comfortable day by the sea.

Culturally, Santorini is rich in heritage. The Museum of Prehistoric Thera in Fira houses an extensive collection of artifacts from Akrotiri, including pottery, tools, and frescoes. This museum offers valuable context to the ancient ruins and provides a deeper understanding of Minoan culture.

When it comes to dining, Santorini offers a range of culinary experiences. For fine dining, Selene in Pyrgos is celebrated for its innovative Greek cuisine using locally sourced ingredients. For a more casual meal, Ammoudi Fish Tavern in Oia serves fresh seafood with a view of the caldera, while Katerina's Restaurant in Fira offers traditional Greek dishes in a charming setting.

Accommodation options on Santorini cater to various preferences. For a luxurious stay, Canaves Oia Hotel offers stunning views of the caldera, private pools, and exceptional service. Katikies Hotel, also in Oia, provides an elegant experience with cliffside rooms and renowned hospitality. For a more budget-friendly option, Santorini Secret Suites & Spa in Oia offers comfortable accommodations with a central location, balancing luxury and affordability.

Santorini, with its combination of dramatic landscapes, rich history, and vibrant culture, promises an unforgettable experience. Whether you're exploring ancient ruins, relaxing on beautiful beaches, or enjoying exquisite local cuisine, the island invites you to immerse yourself in its unique charm and beauty.

Rhodes, Greece

Rhodes, a sun-soaked island in the Eastern Mediterranean, offers a captivating blend of ancient history, stunning landscapes, and vibrant culture. As a popular cruise port, Rhodes provides a range of experiences from exploring medieval fortresses to relaxing on beautiful beaches.

Begin your exploration in Rhodes Town, where the Old Town is a must-see. This UNESCO World Heritage site is a maze of cobblestone streets surrounded by medieval walls. Wander through the historic city and admire the architecture of the Palace of the Grand Master, a formidable fortress that once served as the seat of the Knights Hospitaller. Its grand halls and intricate mosaics offer a glimpse into the island's storied past. Nearby, the Street of the Knights, lined with medieval inns, adds to the historical charm.

Adjacent to the Old Town, the New Town provides a contrast with its lively atmosphere. Visit Mandraki Harbor, the site where the famous Colossus of Rhodes once stood, and enjoy the view of the island's iconic windmills. This area is perfect for a relaxed stroll along the waterfront.

For a dose of ancient history, head to Lindos, located on the southeastern coast of Rhodes. The Acropolis of Lindos, perched atop a rocky promontory, offers spectacular views of the surrounding area and the sea. Explore the ruins, including a well-preserved ancient temple of Athena and remnants from the Hellenistic period.

Outdoor enthusiasts will appreciate Rhodes' natural beauty. The island's coastline features a range of beaches, from the lively Faliraki Beach, known for its water sports and vibrant atmosphere, to the more tranquil Agia Pelagia Beach, which offers golden sands and clear waters. For a taste of nature, hike through the Valley of the Butterflies near the village of Archanes. This lush area is particularly enchanting in summer when thousands of butterflies fill the valley.

Culturally, Rhodes is rich in heritage. The Archaeological Museum of Rhodes, housed in a medieval hospital, showcases artifacts from various periods of the island's history, including sculptures, pottery, and mosaics. Another cultural highlight is the Rhodes Folklore Museum, located in a traditional mansion, which offers insight into local customs, crafts, and daily life on the island.

Dining in Rhodes is a pleasure, with a variety of options to suit different tastes. Mavrikos, in Lindos, is renowned for its inventive Greek cuisine and elegant setting. For a more casual meal, Loukoulos in Rhodes Town offers a range of traditional Greek dishes in a welcoming atmosphere. Seafood enthusiasts should visit Ippokambos, which serves fresh catches with views of the harbor.

Accommodation in Rhodes caters to various preferences. For a luxurious stay, Hotel Rodos Palace offers elegant rooms, a large pool, and extensive facilities. The Atrium Prestige Thalasso Spa Resort & Villas provides a high-end experience with private villas and exceptional spa services. For those on a tighter budget, Hotel Mediterranean offers comfortable accommodations with a central location and easy access to the city and beaches.

Rhodes, with its mix of historical grandeur, natural beauty, and vibrant culture, promises a rich and rewarding experience. Whether exploring ancient ruins, relaxing on idyllic beaches, or savoring local flavors, the island invites you to immerse yourself in its captivating charm.

Heraklion (Crete), Greece

Heraklion, the vibrant capital of Crete, is a gateway to the island's rich history and diverse attractions. As a key port in the Eastern Mediterranean, it offers visitors a fascinating mix of ancient ruins, cultural experiences, and natural beauty.

Begin your exploration with a trip to the Knossos Palace, one of the most significant archaeological sites in Greece. Just a short drive from Heraklion, this ancient Minoan palace complex is renowned for its intricate frescoes and labyrinthine layout. As you explore the ruins, imagine life in this ancient civilization and marvel at the elaborate artworks that have been preserved over millennia.

Back in the city, the Heraklion Archaeological Museum provides a deeper understanding of the Minoan civilization. This museum boasts one of the most comprehensive collections of Minoan artifacts, including sculptures, pottery, and jewelry. The exhibits offer valuable context to the artifacts discovered at Knossos and shed light on the island's historical significance.

Another historical highlight is the Venetian Walls, which encircle the city. Built during the Venetian rule in the 16th century, these formidable fortifications offer panoramic views of Heraklion and its surroundings. Nearby, the Koules Fortress at the harbor stands as a testament to the city's medieval past and provides stunning vistas of the sea.

For a taste of local life, visit the Central Market in Heraklion. Here, you'll find a bustling array of fresh produce, cheeses, and spices. The market is a vibrant place to experience the city's daily rhythm and sample local flavors.

Outdoor enthusiasts will find plenty to enjoy around Heraklion. Hersonissos Beach, located to the east of the city, is known for its lively atmosphere and range of water sports. For a quieter retreat, head to Agia Pelagia Beach, which offers clear waters and a more serene environment. Nature lovers might also enjoy exploring the Gorge of the Dead near Archanes, where scenic hiking trails reveal the island's rugged terrain.

Crete's rich culinary tradition is reflected in Heraklion's dining scene. Peskesi is a standout restaurant offering modern interpretations of traditional Cretan dishes, using fresh, local ingredients. For a more casual meal, Loukoulos provides a cozy setting and a variety of classic Greek dishes. Seafood lovers should not miss Ippokambos, which offers fresh catches with views of the harbor.

Accommodation in Heraklion ranges from luxurious to budget-friendly options. Aquila Atlantis Hotel, located centrally, offers stylish rooms, a rooftop pool, and excellent service. Galaxy Iraklio Hotel provides a blend of modern amenities and traditional charm. For a more affordable stay, Kastro Hotel offers comfortable rooms in a central location.

Dubrovnik, Croatia

Dubrovnik, often referred to as the "Pearl of the Adriatic," is a stunning destination on Croatia's southeastern coast, offering a blend of historical grandeur and natural beauty. As a prominent cruise port in the Eastern Mediterranean, Dubrovnik attracts visitors with its well-preserved medieval architecture, picturesque harbor, and vibrant local culture.

Start your exploration with a stroll through Dubrovnik's Old Town, a UNESCO World Heritage site encircled by imposing city walls. Wander along the Stradun, the main thoroughfare lined with historic buildings and bustling shops. The Old Town's labyrinthine streets reveal charming squares, ancient churches, and historic landmarks. Don't miss the chance to walk the City Walls, which offer breathtaking views of the Adriatic Sea and the terracotta roofs of the Old Town.

The Rector's Palace is another must-see attraction. This Renaissance building once served as the administrative center of the Dubrovnik Republic and now houses the Cultural Historical Museum. Explore its ornate rooms, period furniture, and artifacts that provide insight into Dubrovnik's storied past.

For a taste of local culture, visit the Dubrovnik Cathedral. Located on the site of an earlier Byzantine church, this baroque cathedral features impressive architecture and a treasury filled with religious relics and artifacts. Nearby, the Sponza Palace, a historic building that once served as a customs house and treasury, is now home to the Dubrovnik State Archives.

Outdoor enthusiasts will find plenty to enjoy in and around Dubrovnik. Take a cable car ride up to Mount Srdj for panoramic views of the city and the surrounding coastline. At the summit, there's also a restaurant where you can relax and take in the scenery. For a more serene experience, explore Lokrum Island, a short boat ride from the city. The island features beautiful gardens, historic ruins, and secluded beaches, making it a perfect spot for a leisurely day trip.

Dubrovnik's coastline offers several inviting beaches. Banje Beach, located just outside the city walls, is known for its clear waters and stunning views of the Old Town. For a quieter experience, head to Sveti Jakov Beach, a pebble beach with a more relaxed atmosphere and beautiful surroundings.

When it comes to dining, Dubrovnik has a diverse culinary scene. For fine dining, try Nautika, which offers exquisite seafood dishes and spectacular views of the city's walls and the sea. For a more casual meal, head to Konoba Dubrava, known for its traditional Croatian cuisine and charming setting. Another excellent choice is Bota Sushi & Oyster Bar, which combines fresh seafood with a creative menu.

Accommodation in Dubrovnik caters to various tastes and budgets. For luxury, the Hotel Excelsior provides elegant rooms with stunning sea views and top-notch amenities. The Hilton Imperial Dubrovnik, located near the Old Town, offers a blend of modern comfort and historic charm. For a more budget-friendly option, the Hotel Kompas offers comfortable accommodations and easy access to both the city and the beach.

Dubrovnik's enchanting blend of historical splendor, cultural richness, and natural beauty ensures a memorable visit. Whether you're exploring ancient streets, relaxing on beautiful beaches, or savoring local cuisine, the city promises a captivating experience in one of the Mediterranean's most picturesque settings.

Split, Croatia

Split, a vibrant coastal city in Croatia, is a gateway to both historical wonders and natural beauty. As one of the key ports in the Eastern Mediterranean, Split offers visitors a rich tapestry of experiences, from ancient Roman architecture to scenic waterfronts and lively local culture.

Begin your exploration with the heart of Split—the Diocletian's Palace. This sprawling Roman complex, built in the 4th century, forms the core of the Old Town. Wander through its labyrinthine streets, where ancient walls and historic buildings blend seamlessly with modern shops, cafes, and restaurants. Key highlights within the palace include the Peristyle, a grand courtyard surrounded by columns, and the Cathedral of Saint Domnius, which was originally built as Diocletian's mausoleum. Climbing the cathedral's bell tower offers panoramic views of the city and the Adriatic Sea.

A short walk from the palace leads to the Riva, Split's with cafes and restaurants where you can enjoy a coffee or a meal while soaking in the atmosphere.

For a taste of Split's rich history, visit the Archaeological Museum, which houses an extensive collection of artifacts from prehistoric times through the Roman period. The museum's exhibits include ancient coins, pottery, and sculptures, providing a comprehensive overview of the region's past.

Outdoor enthusiasts will find plenty to enjoy in Split. Marjan Hill, located on the peninsula just west of the city center, is a green oasis offering scenic walking and hiking trails. The hill provides stunning views of the city and the surrounding islands, and its shaded paths are perfect for a relaxing escape from the urban bustle.

Split's coastline features several inviting beaches. Bacvice Beach, located near the city center, is popular for its sandy shore and shallow waters, making it ideal for swimming and sunbathing. For a more tranquil experience, head to Kasjuni Beach, which offers a more serene atmosphere and clear waters, perfect for a peaceful retreat.

Dining in Split offers a variety of options, from traditional Croatian fare to international cuisine. For an authentic experience, try Konoba Fetivi, a family-run restaurant known for its seafood and traditional Dalmatian dishes. Another excellent choice is Bistro Toc, which serves modern Mediterranean cuisine in a cozy setting. For a taste of Italy, visit Pizzeria Galija, which offers delicious pizzas and a welcoming atmosphere.

Accommodation in Split caters to various preferences and budgets. For luxury, the Hotel Park Split offers elegant rooms, a beautiful location near the beach, and excellent amenities. The Radisson Blu Resort & Spa provides upscale accommodations with stunning sea views and a range of facilities, including a spa and outdoor pool. For a more budget-friendly option, Hotel Marmont provides comfortable accommodations with a central location, making it easy to explore the city on foot.

Split's blend of historical charm, natural beauty, and vibrant local culture ensures a memorable visit. Whether you're exploring ancient ruins, relaxing on picturesque beaches, or enjoying local cuisine, the city offers a diverse range of experiences in a stunning Mediterranean setting.

Kotor, Montenegro

Kotor, nestled along Montenegro's Adriatic coast, is a stunning destination where medieval charm meets breathtaking natural beauty. This historic town, encased within ancient fortifications and set against the dramatic backdrop of the Bay of Kotor, offers a unique blend of history, culture, and outdoor adventure.

Start your visit with a wander through the Old Town of Kotor, a UNESCO World Heritage site. Its maze of narrow cobblestone streets, lined with well-preserved medieval buildings, creates an enchanting atmosphere. Key landmarks include the Cathedral of Saint Tryphon, a Romanesque church renowned for its intricate carvings and historical significance. Just a short walk away, the Maritime Museum of Kotor provides insight into the town's maritime history, showcasing a collection of models, maps, and maritime artifacts.

No visit to Kotor is complete without a hike up to the Kotor Fortress, also known as San Giovanni Fortress. This formidable structure, perched high on a hill, offers a rewarding climb with spectacular views over the bay and the town below. The fortress was originally built in the 9th century and expanded over the centuries. The trek up the 1,350 steps is both a physical challenge and a journey through history, with panoramic vistas serving as a perfect payoff.

For outdoor enthusiasts, Kotor's bay and surrounding landscapes provide ample opportunities. The Bay of Kotor itself is a natural wonder, with crystal-clear waters and dramatic fjord-like scenery. Take a boat tour to explore the bay and its quaint islands, such as Our Lady of the Rocks, a man-made island with a small church and museum that tells the story of local maritime traditions.

The nearby Lovćen National Park offers a chance to explore Montenegro's rugged interior. The park features a network of trails, including those leading to the mausoleum of Petar II Petrović Njegoš, a key figure in Montenegrin history. The views from the mausoleum are among the most stunning in the country, providing sweeping vistas of the surrounding mountains and valleys.

Kotor's dining scene reflects its Mediterranean heritage, with a range of restaurants offering fresh local cuisine. For an authentic experience, visit Konoba Catovica Mlini, a charming restaurant located in a restored mill, known for its seafood and traditional Montenegrin dishes. Another excellent choice is the Old Town Restaurant, where you can enjoy a variety of Mediterranean dishes in a picturesque setting. For a more casual meal, try the Gallo Nero, which serves delicious pizza and pasta in a relaxed atmosphere.

Accommodation in Kotor varies from luxury to budget options. For a luxurious stay, the Hotel Forza Terra offers elegant rooms with views of the bay and top-notch amenities. The Hotel Astoria, located in the heart of the Old Town, provides a blend of historic charm and modern comfort. For more budget-friendly options, the Montenegro Hostel B&B offers comfortable accommodations with a central location, making it easy to explore the town.

Kotor, with its mix of medieval charm, natural beauty, and rich cultural heritage, provides a captivating experience for travelers. Whether you're exploring ancient fortifications, hiking through stunning landscapes, or savoring local cuisine, this enchanting town promises a memorable visit in one of the most picturesque settings of the Eastern Mediterranean.

Istanbul, Turkey

Istanbul, straddling the divide between Europe and Asia, is a city of extraordinary contrasts and rich history. As Turkey's largest city and a pivotal port in the Eastern Mediterranean, it offers travelers an array of experiences that blend ancient heritage with vibrant modernity. Whether you're interested in exploring historic sites, indulging in local cuisine, or experiencing the city's lively cultural scene, Istanbul provides a compelling adventure for every visitor.

Start your exploration in Sultanahmet, the heart of Istanbul's historical district. The Hagia Sophia, a former cathedral turned mosque and now a museum, stands as a testament to the city's diverse history. Its vast dome and intricate mosaics reflect both Byzantine and Ottoman influences, making it a must-see landmark. Nearby, the Blue Mosque, with its striking blue tiles and six minarets, offers a glimpse into Ottoman architectural grandeur.

Just a short walk away is the Topkapi Palace, the former residence of Ottoman sultans. The palace complex includes opulent courtyards, lush gardens, and a treasury filled with priceless artifacts. The Harem section, with its richly decorated rooms, provides insight into the private lives of the sultans and their families.

A visit to the Basilica Cistern, an underground marvel supported by hundreds of columns, reveals a different aspect of Istanbul's history. The dimly lit cavernous space, with its reflective waters and atmospheric lighting, offers a unique perspective on Byzantine engineering.

For a taste of local life and vibrant commerce, head to the Grand Bazaar. This sprawling market is a labyrinth of shops selling everything from intricate carpets and jewelry to spices and textiles. The bazaar's lively atmosphere and diverse range of goods make it a fascinating place to explore. The nearby Spice Bazaar offers a more concentrated experience of aromatic herbs, teas, and sweets.

To experience Istanbul's outdoor beauty, take a stroll along the Bosphorus. A ferry ride along this strait provides stunning views of the city's skyline and landmarks such as the Dolmabahçe Palace and the Bosphorus Bridge. Alternatively, a walk through the Emirgan Park during spring reveals lush gardens and beautiful tulip displays.

Istanbul's cultural scene is equally captivating. The Istanbul Modern Art Museum showcases contemporary Turkish art in a striking building on the waterfront. For a more traditional experience, the Turkish and Islamic Arts Museum offers an extensive collection of calligraphy, ceramics, and textiles.

Dining in Istanbul is a treat for the senses. For an authentic experience, visit a local meyhane (tavern) like Asitane, which serves traditional Ottoman dishes with a modern twist. For seafood lovers, the restaurant Balikçi Sabahattin offers fresh fish in a charming, old-world setting. For a more casual meal, Çiya Sofrası in Kadıköy provides an array of regional Turkish specialties that highlight the country's diverse culinary traditions.

Accommodation options in Istanbul cater to various preferences. The Four Seasons Hotel Istanbul at Sultanahmet offers luxurious accommodations with views of the Hagia Sophia and the Blue Mosque. For a more boutique experience, the Hotel Amira offers charming rooms and personalized service in a central location. Budget travelers will appreciate the Sultanahmet Palace Hotel, which provides comfortable rooms and proximity to major attractions.

CHAPTER 6
ADRIATIC PORTS

The Adriatic Sea, with its crystal-clear waters and dramatic coastal landscapes, is a treasure trove of stunning ports and charming destinations. Stretching from the northern reaches of Italy down to the southern shores of Albania, this enchanting stretch of the Mediterranean offers a rich tapestry of history, culture, and natural beauty. As you journey through the Adriatic ports, you'll uncover a mosaic of experiences that capture the essence of this captivating region.

The Adriatic coastline is renowned for its striking contrasts—from the historic grandeur of ancient cities to the serene allure of secluded beaches. Each port along this route has its unique character, shaped by centuries of history and diverse cultural influences. The ancient and modern blend seamlessly in these ports, creating a vibrant atmosphere that enchants every traveler.

Begin your exploration in the enchanting city of Dubrovnik, a UNESCO World Heritage site that gleams with medieval charm. The city's well-preserved walls, cobblestone streets, and historic buildings offer a glimpse into its illustrious past as a powerful maritime republic. Wander through its maze-like Old Town, and you'll find yourself immersed in its rich history and picturesque scenery.

Further up the coast, Split presents a fascinating blend of ancient and contemporary life. The city is anchored by Diocletian's Palace, a Roman marvel that has been seamlessly integrated into the modern urban fabric. As you stroll through the bustling streets of Split, you'll experience the lively atmosphere of its markets, cafes, and waterfront promenades, all set against a backdrop of historic splendor.

The charming city of Kotor, nestled within the dramatic fjord-like Bay of Kotor, offers a different kind of allure. Surrounded by steep mountains and ancient fortifications, Kotor's medieval Old Town is a labyrinth of narrow streets, historic churches, and scenic squares. The city's blend of natural beauty and well-preserved architecture makes it a picturesque stop on your Adriatic voyage.

Another gem of the Adriatic is the vibrant port city of Mykonos, known for its lively nightlife, stunning beaches, and distinctive whitewashed architecture. The island's blend of cosmopolitan flair and traditional charm provides a unique contrast to the historical cities of the region, offering both relaxation and excitement in equal measure.

Crete's Heraklion, a bustling hub of activity and history, serves as a gateway to the island's rich Minoan heritage. The nearby archaeological sites, such as the ancient Palace of Knossos, provide a fascinating insight into one of Europe's earliest civilizations. Heraklion itself is a vibrant city with a blend of modern amenities and historical landmarks.

Each port along the Adriatic is a testament to the rich and diverse history of this region. From the ancient ruins of Roman emperors to the medieval fortifications of powerful city-states, these destinations offer a journey through time, filled with captivating stories and breathtaking landscapes. Whether you're exploring historic sites, savoring local cuisine, or simply enjoying the stunning natural beauty of the Adriatic coast, this journey promises to be an unforgettable adventure.

Venice, Italian

Venice, a city like no other, floats gracefully on its network of canals and islands, weaving a timeless charm that enchants every traveler. Known as the "City of Canals," Venice offers a unique experience with its labyrinth of waterways, historic buildings, and artistic heritage. This magical city, with its rich history and vibrant culture, is a destination where every corner reveals a new marvel.

Begin your exploration at the iconic Piazza San Marco, often considered the heart of Venice. This grand square is flanked by stunning architectural masterpieces, including the magnificent St. Mark's Basilica. The basilica's opulent facade and intricately designed mosaics are a testament to the city's artistic and religious heritage. Adjacent to the basilica stands the Campanile di San Marco, a bell tower offering panoramic views of the city's sprawling network of canals and islands.

A short stroll from Piazza San Marco brings you to the Doge's Palace, a masterpiece of Gothic architecture that once served as the residence of the Venetian Doge. The palace's richly decorated rooms and grand halls, including the famous Hall of the Great Council, offer a glimpse into the opulence and political history of Venice. Don't miss a walk across the Bridge of Sighs, which connects the palace to the former prison, offering a poignant view of the city through its barred windows.

To truly experience Venice, a gondola ride through its serene canals is a must. Gliding along the Grand Canal, you'll be treated to a unique perspective of the city's palatial facades and charming bridges. For a more immersive experience, explore the narrower canals where you can admire the hidden corners and quiet charm of Venetian residential life.

Venturing beyond the well-trodden paths of central Venice, the islands of Murano, Burano, and Torcello offer delightful excursions. Murano is renowned for its exquisite glass-blowing artistry, with numerous workshops and galleries showcasing this traditional craft. Burano, with its brightly colored houses and intricate lacework, provides a picturesque setting perfect for leisurely exploration. Torcello, one of the oldest Venetian settlements, features historic sites such as the Church of Santa Maria Assunta and its stunning Byzantine mosaics.

The cultural richness of Venice is also reflected in its museums and art galleries. The Gallerie dell'Accademia houses an impressive collection of Venetian Renaissance art, while the Peggy Guggenheim Collection offers a modern art perspective in a beautiful canal-side palace.

Venice's dining scene is a culinary journey of its own. For a taste of local Venetian cuisine, head to Osteria alle Testiere, a cozy eatery known for its seafood dishes and intimate ambiance. For a more casual meal, the trattoria Da Fiore offers traditional Venetian fare in a welcoming setting. If you're in the mood for something sweet, don't miss trying a traditional tiramisu at one of the city's charming cafes.

Accommodation options in Venice range from luxurious hotels to charming boutique stays. The Bauer Palazzo, located near St. Mark's Square, offers opulent rooms with stunning canal views. The Gritti Palace, a former noble residence, combines historic charm with modern luxury. For a more budget-friendly option, the Hotel Antiche Figure provides comfortable accommodations with easy access to the city's main attractions.

Venice, with its enchanting canals, historic landmarks, and rich cultural heritage, promises an unforgettable experience. Whether you're wandering through its historic squares, cruising its serene waterways, or indulging in its culinary delights, Venice invites you to immerse yourself in its timeless allure.

Bari, Italy

Bari, a vibrant port city on the Adriatic Sea, is a gateway to the rich history and culture of southern Italy. As the capital of the Puglia region, Bari offers a captivating mix of historical landmarks, picturesque seaside views, and lively local traditions. The city's blend of ancient charm and modern vibrancy makes it an enticing destination for travelers seeking both cultural exploration and leisurely relaxation.

Begin your visit in the heart of Bari's historic center, known as Bari Vecchia. This maze of narrow, winding streets is home to some of the city's most significant landmarks. At the center of this area stands the Basilica of Saint Nicholas, an important pilgrimage site that houses the relics of Saint Nicholas, the patron saint of Bari. The basilica's Romanesque architecture and serene interior make it a must-see.

Nearby, you'll find the Castello Normanno-Svevo, a formidable Norman castle that has stood guard over Bari for centuries. The castle's imposing walls and towers offer a glimpse into its past as a military fortress. Explore its interior to uncover exhibitions on the city's history and enjoy panoramic views from its ramparts.

For a taste of local life, stroll along the Lungomare, Bari's scenic waterfront promenade. This lively stretch is perfect for a leisurely walk, offering views of the sparkling Adriatic Sea and the bustling harbor. Along the way, you'll find charming cafes and gelaterias where you can savor local delicacies and enjoy the sea breeze.

Bari is also known for its traditional cuisine, and exploring its local food scene is a delightful experience. Sample authentic Pugliese dishes at Osteria Le Arpie, a cozy eatery renowned for its homemade pasta and rustic flavors. For a more upscale dining experience, try Ristorante Biancorosso, which offers a refined menu featuring local seafood and regional specialties.

The city's cultural scene is vibrant and varied. The Teatro Petruzzelli, one of Italy's largest and most prestigious opera houses, hosts a range of performances from classical music to contemporary theater. Check the schedule during your visit to catch a live performance in this grand historic venue.

Outdoor enthusiasts will appreciate the nearby natural beauty. Just outside Bari, the coastal town of Polignano a Mare is famous for its dramatic cliffs and crystal-clear waters. Explore its scenic beaches and dramatic sea caves or take a boat tour to fully appreciate its stunning coastline.

Accommodation options in Bari cater to a range of preferences and budgets. For a luxurious stay, consider the Palace Hotel Bari, located near the city center and offering elegant rooms and excellent amenities. The Grande Albergo delle Nazioni, with its stunning sea views and refined atmosphere, provides a touch of opulence. For a more budget-friendly choice, the Hotel Boston offers comfortable accommodations with easy access to the city's main attractions.

Bari, with its rich history, vibrant culture, and scenic beauty, offers an enriching and enjoyable experience. From its historic landmarks and lively promenades to its delectable cuisine and nearby natural wonders, the city invites travelers to immerse themselves in its unique charm and discover the many facets of southern Italy.

Koper, Slovenia

Koper, Slovenia's largest port city, presents a delightful blend of historical charm and modern vibrancy on the Adriatic coast. Nestled between Italy and Croatia, Koper boasts a rich maritime heritage, picturesque streets, and a warm Mediterranean ambiance. Its compact size and welcoming atmosphere make it an ideal destination for a leisurely exploration.

Begin your visit in the heart of Koper's Old Town, where narrow, cobblestone streets are lined with colorful facades and historic buildings. Tito Square serves as the central hub of the city, surrounded by notable landmarks including the Praetorian Palace. This Renaissance gem, with its ornate façade and intricate details, once served as the residence of Venetian governors. Adjacent to the palace is the Koper Cathedral, a blend of Romanesque and Gothic styles. Its bell tower offers panoramic views of the city and surrounding coast.

A short stroll from the square will lead you to the Regional Museum of Koper, housed in a former Jesuit monastery. The museum's exhibits cover the city's history from ancient times through the Venetian era and beyond, providing valuable context to Koper's past and cultural evolution.

For a taste of Koper's seaside charm, explore the Marina and Waterfront area. The bustling promenade is perfect for a leisurely walk, offering views of the Adriatic Sea and the city's colorful harbor. Here, you can enjoy a coffee or gelato at one of the waterfront cafes and watch the boats come and go.

Outdoor enthusiasts will find plenty to enjoy in and around Koper. Just a short drive from the city, the Škocjan Caves, a UNESCO World Heritage site, offer a stunning underground adventure. Explore the vast caverns and subterranean rivers of this impressive natural wonder. Another nearby attraction is the Debeli Rtič Nature Reserve, known for its scenic walking trails and tranquil coastal scenery.

Koper's culinary scene reflects its Mediterranean influences, with numerous dining options that showcase local and regional flavors. Fritolin pri Cantini is a popular spot for fresh seafood and traditional Slovenian dishes in a casual setting. For a more refined dining experience, Restavracija Nino offers a sophisticated menu that combines Slovenian and international cuisine, accompanied by excellent local wines.

Accommodation in Koper ranges from luxury to budget-friendly options. Hotel Koper, situated near the city center and waterfront, offers comfortable rooms and convenient amenities. For a more upscale stay, Hotel Marina provides stylish accommodations with beautiful views of the marina and the Adriatic Sea. Budget travelers can opt for Hotel Vodno, which offers clean, affordable rooms and is a short distance from the city's main attractions.

Koper, with its blend of historical allure, scenic beauty, and vibrant local culture, provides a memorable experience for travelers. Whether you're exploring ancient sites, enjoying the seaside promenade, or savoring local cuisine, Koper invites you to immerse yourself in its unique charm and discover the essence of Slovenia's Adriatic coast.

Zadar, Croatia

Zadar, a historic city on Croatia's Adriatic coast, offers a captivating mix of ancient ruins, vibrant city life, and natural beauty. Known for its stunning sunsets and unique coastal charm, Zadar is a treasure trove for travelers seeking a blend of historical exploration and modern relaxation.

Start your exploration in Zadar's Old Town, where Roman and Venetian influences intertwine with contemporary life. The city is home to the impressive Roman Forum, situated in the heart of the Old Town. This ancient site, surrounded by columns and remnants of historic buildings, offers a glimpse into Zadar's past as a significant Roman settlement. Nearby, the St. Donatus Church stands out with its circular shape and historical significance, dating back to the 9th century. The church, once a Byzantine basilica, now serves as a venue for music concerts and offers a striking contrast to its surroundings.

A short walk from the Forum leads to the Sea Organ, an innovative installation that uses the movement of the sea to produce musical sounds. This unique attraction, designed by architect Nikola Bašić, is a must-see, especially during sunset when the combination of sound and color creates a mesmerizing experience. Right next to the Sea Organ, the Greeting to the Sun is another of Bašić's creations. This large, circular solar panel installation absorbs sunlight during the day and illuminates the night with colorful light displays.

Outdoor enthusiasts will appreciate Zadar's natural beauty. The city is a gateway to some of Croatia's most stunning islands and national parks. Take a boat trip to the nearby Kornati National Park, known for its rugged beauty and crystal-clear waters. Another great destination is the Paklenica National Park, renowned for its dramatic canyons and hiking trails that cater to various skill levels.

Zadar's culinary scene reflects its coastal location, offering fresh seafood and Mediterranean flavors. For a delightful dining experience, try Foša, a restaurant known for its excellent seafood and elegant atmosphere. For a more relaxed setting, Konoba Skoblar offers traditional Croatian dishes and a cozy ambiance. Pizzeria La Dolce Vita is a great spot for a casual meal, serving a variety of pizzas and Italian favorites.

Accommodation in Zadar ranges from luxurious to budget-friendly options. The Falkensteiner Hotel & Spa Iadera offers a high-end experience with stunning sea views, a luxurious spa, and fine dining options. For a more moderate stay, Hotel Bastion provides comfortable accommodations with a central location and easy access to the city's main attractions. Budget travelers may opt for Hotel Kolovare, which offers clean rooms and a convenient location near the beach and city center.

Zadar's blend of historical allure, scenic beauty, and vibrant culture creates a memorable experience for visitors. Whether exploring ancient ruins, enjoying coastal views, or indulging in local cuisine, Zadar invites you to immerse yourself in its unique charm and discover the essence of Croatia's Adriatic coast.

Corfu, Greece

Corfu, a lush island in the Ionian Sea, captivates visitors with its rich history, vibrant culture, and stunning landscapes. Known for its charming old town, beautiful beaches, and verdant hills, Corfu offers a delightful blend of historical exploration and natural beauty.

Begin your exploration in Corfu Town, a UNESCO World Heritage Site that showcases a unique blend of Venetian, French, and British influences. Wander through the narrow streets and discover the Old Fortress, a formidable structure that offers panoramic views of the town and surrounding sea. The New Fortress, located to the west, provides further insight into the island's military history and offers more spectacular vistas.

One of the town's highlights is the Liston Promenade, an elegant arcaded walkway that reflects French architectural influence. It's a great place to enjoy a coffee or take a leisurely stroll while soaking in the historic atmosphere. Nearby, the Saint Spyridon Church is an important religious site and a must-see for its ornate interior and historical significance.

Corfu is also known for its stunning natural beauty. Head to the Achilleion Palace, built by Empress of Austria, Elisabeth of Bavaria. The palace, surrounded by beautiful gardens, offers a glimpse into the opulent lifestyle of its former owner and provides magnificent views of the surrounding countryside.

For outdoor enthusiasts, the island offers numerous opportunities for exploration. The Mount Pantokrator area is ideal for hiking, providing panoramic views of the island and the Ionian Sea. The nearby village of Paleokastritsa, with its crystal-clear waters and dramatic coastline, is perfect for swimming and boat trips. Don't miss the opportunity to visit the Corfu Archaeological Museum, which houses a collection of artifacts from the island's ancient past, including items from the nearby Temple of Artemis.

Corfu's culinary scene reflects its diverse cultural influences. For an authentic taste of local cuisine, try taverna The Venetian Well, which offers traditional dishes in a charming setting. Another popular spot is Avli, known for its fresh seafood and relaxed atmosphere. If you're in the mood for something casual, head to

Pizzeria La Tavola, which serves delicious pizzas and Italian favorites.

Accommodation options in Corfu cater to a variety of preferences and budgets. For a luxurious stay, the Corfu Imperial, Grecotel Exclusive Resort provides elegant rooms, stunning views, and top-notch amenities. The Mayor Mon Repos Palace is a more moderate choice, offering comfortable accommodations with easy access to both the town and the beach. Budget travelers will find the Hotel Atlantis to be a good option, with clean rooms and a convenient location near the city center.

Corfu, with its blend of historical richness, natural beauty, and vibrant culture, offers a memorable experience for every traveler. Whether you're exploring ancient sites, enjoying scenic landscapes, or savoring local flavors, Corfu invites you to immerse yourself in its unique charm and discover the essence of Greece's Adriatic coast.

CHAPTER 7
AEGEAN AND BLACK SEA PORT

The Aegean and Black Sea ports offer a captivating journey through some of the most historically and culturally rich regions of Europe and Asia. This chapter takes you through the vibrant landscapes and storied pasts of these areas, where ancient civilizations, stunning coastlines, and modern cities converge in a mesmerizing blend of experiences. From the sun-drenched shores of the Aegean to the historic harbors of the Black Sea, each port in this region provides a unique glimpse into its local heritage, natural beauty, and dynamic present.

The Aegean Sea, stretching between the southeastern coast of Greece and the western shores of Turkey, is renowned for its crystal-clear waters, idyllic islands, and ancient ruins. The Greek islands, including iconic destinations like Santorini and Mykonos, offer travelers breathtaking views, whitewashed buildings, and a sense of timeless charm. These islands are not just picturesque; they are steeped in mythology and history, with ruins and artifacts that narrate tales from ancient Greece. The Turkish coast, with its ports such as Kusadasi and Bodrum, complements this allure with its rich history, including significant sites like Ephesus and the Mausoleum at Halicarnassus.

The Black Sea, lying to the northeast of the Aegean, is bordered by a diverse range of countries, each contributing its own cultural and historical layers to this unique maritime region. The ports along the Black Sea, such as Istanbul and Varna, are gateways to explore a fascinating mix of Eastern and Western influences. Istanbul, straddling the divide between Europe and Asia, is a city where ancient empires have left their mark, evident in its stunning architecture, bustling markets, and vibrant street life. Varna, Bulgaria's Black Sea capital, is known for its beautiful beaches and its role in the region's history, with sites ranging from ancient Roman baths to contemporary cultural institutions.

Venturing into the Aegean and Black Sea ports offers a journey through time and culture, from the ancient ruins of classical civilizations to the lively modern cities that thrive today. The rich tapestry of history, combined with the scenic beauty of these coastal regions, creates an enchanting destination for travelers seeking both relaxation and discovery. Whether you are drawn to the historic ruins of ancient Greece and Rome, the bustling bazaars of Istanbul, or the serene beaches of Bulgaria, the Aegean and Black Sea ports promise an unforgettable adventure filled with cultural insights, natural wonders, and historical exploration.

Thessaloniki, Greece

Thessaloniki, Greece's vibrant second city, sits nestled between the Aegean Sea and the foothills of Mount Chortiatis. This bustling port city, rich in history and culture, is a captivating blend of ancient ruins, lively urban life, and picturesque coastal scenery. As a gateway to the northern regions of Greece, Thessaloniki offers a diverse array of experiences for travelers, making it an exciting destination on the Aegean and Black Sea routes.

Start your exploration at the White Tower, the city's most iconic landmark. This 15th-century Byzantine fortress stands proudly on the waterfront and provides panoramic views of Thessaloniki and the Aegean Sea. It houses the Museum of Byzantine Culture, which showcases the region's rich Byzantine history through its extensive collection of artifacts, including mosaics, sculptures, and manuscripts.

Nearby, the Rotunda, an impressive cylindrical building originally constructed as a mausoleum for the Roman Emperor Galerius, is another must-see. Over the centuries, it has served as a Christian church and a mosque, reflecting the city's diverse past. The interior boasts magnificent mosaics and frescoes that are well worth a visit.

Wander through the Ano Poli, the old town of Thessaloniki, where you'll find charming, narrow streets lined with traditional houses and stunning views of the city. This area retains much of its historical character, providing a picturesque contrast to the bustling modern parts of Thessaloniki.

For outdoor enthusiasts, the city's waterfront promenade is a perfect place for a leisurely stroll. The recently renovated area stretches for several kilometers along the coast, offering beautiful views of the sea and the chance to relax in one of the many cafes and bars. The nearby Aristotelous Square is a bustling hub, ideal for people-watching and experiencing the lively atmosphere of the city.

Thessaloniki's cultural scene is vibrant and varied. The city's many museums, such as the Archaeological Museum of Thessaloniki, present an extensive collection of artifacts from Macedonia, including items from the ancient city of Aigai, the burial site of the Macedonian kings. The city's vibrant street art and graffiti offer a modern contrast to its historical sites, adding to its unique character.

Dining in Thessaloniki is a delightful experience. For traditional Greek cuisine, head to Modiano Market, where you can sample a variety of local specialties. For a more upscale dining experience, try La Place, known for its sophisticated menu featuring Greek and Mediterranean dishes. The city's numerous tavernas and cafes offer everything from fresh seafood to rich, hearty stews.

Accommodation in Thessaloniki caters to all preferences. The Electra Palace Hotel, located in the heart of the city, offers luxurious rooms and stunning views of the sea. For a more boutique experience, consider the City Hotel Thessaloniki, which combines modern comfort with a central location. Budget travelers can find affordable yet comfortable options at the Hotel Ilios, which provides convenient access to the city's attractions.

Kusadasi (Ephesus), Turkey

Kusadasi, a lively port town on Turkey's Aegean coast, serves as a gateway to the ancient city of Ephesus, one of the most well-preserved archaeological sites in the world. This picturesque destination blends modern amenities with historical grandeur, offering travelers a unique combination of cultural exploration and seaside relaxation.

Start your visit with a trip to Ephesus, located just a short drive from Kusadasi. This ancient city, once a thriving center of commerce and culture, features remarkable ruins that transport visitors back to its heyday. The Library of Celsus stands out as one of the most iconic structures, with its elaborate facade and impressive size. Nearby, the Great Theater, capable of seating up to 25,000 spectators, offers a glimpse into the grandeur of ancient performances and public gatherings. Don't miss the Temple of Artemis, one of the Seven Wonders of the Ancient World, which, although only ruins remain, evokes the temple's former splendor.

In Kusadasi itself, the Kusadasi Castle provides a panoramic view of the harbor and the town. This 13th-century fortress, built by the Genoese, offers insights into the region's medieval past and a lovely vantage point for photographs. Strolling through the town, you'll find the Kusadasi Marina, a bustling area full of shops, cafes, and bars, perfect for a leisurely walk or a sunset drink.

Outdoor enthusiasts will enjoy the nearby Ladies Beach (Kadınlar Plajı), a popular spot for sunbathing and swimming with its clear waters and sandy shore. For a more natural escape, visit Dilek Peninsula-Büyük Menderes Delta National Park, known for its stunning landscapes, hiking trails, and diverse flora and fauna. The park's beaches and walking paths offer a tranquil retreat from the bustling town.

Cultural experiences in Kusadasi include visiting the Ephesus Archaeological Museum in the town center, which houses artifacts uncovered from the Ephesus site, such as sculptures, pottery, and mosaics. Additionally, exploring the local bazaars and markets provides a taste of Turkish culture and craftsmanship, with plenty of opportunities to purchase local goods and souvenirs.

Dining in Kusadasi is a pleasure for the palate. Kofteci Yusuf offers delicious traditional Turkish meatballs and other local specialties in a casual setting. For a more refined dining experience, Mezze Grill serves a variety of grilled dishes and mezze plates with a focus on fresh, high-quality ingredients. Seafood enthusiasts will appreciate Sea Horse Restaurant, known for its fresh catches and beautiful views of the harbor.

Accommodation in Kusadasi caters to various preferences. Korumar Hotel De Luxe provides a luxurious stay with its upscale amenities and stunning sea views. For a more boutique experience, Ilayda Avantgarde Hotel offers stylish accommodations with a central location and modern comforts. Budget-conscious travelers can opt for Hotel Rosy, which provides clean, simple rooms and is conveniently located near the town's attractions.

Kusadasi, with its rich historical significance and vibrant modern life, offers a well-rounded experience for travelers. From the ancient wonders of Ephesus to the charming local culture, this Aegean port city promises a memorable visit filled with exploration, relaxation, and delightful culinary experiences.

Varna, Bulgaria

Varna, Bulgaria's vibrant port city on the Black Sea, is a blend of rich history, cultural depth, and seaside allure. Known as the "Sea Capital of Bulgaria," Varna offers a captivating mix of ancient ruins, beautiful beaches, and bustling urban life. Its unique position on the Black Sea coast makes it an ideal destination for travelers seeking both historical exploration and coastal relaxation.

Begin your visit with a trip to the Varna Archaeological Museum, which houses a wealth of artifacts from the region's past, including the famous Gold of Varna, the oldest gold treasure in the world. The museum's extensive collection provides insight into the area's history from prehistoric times through the Roman period and beyond.

Stroll through the city center to discover the Cathedral of the Assumption, a striking example of Byzantine architecture with its grand domes and intricate frescoes. The cathedral is not only a place of worship but also a key landmark in Varna's skyline.

A must-see for any visitor is the Roman Baths of Varna, one of the largest and best-preserved Roman bath complexes in the Balkans. The site offers a glimpse into the grandeur of ancient Roman leisure and is a fascinating contrast to the modern city surrounding it.

For outdoor activities, head to the Sea Garden (Morska Gradina), Varna's expansive park that stretches along the coast. It's an ideal spot for a leisurely walk or picnic, offering scenic views of the Black Sea and a variety of attractions, including a botanical garden, a dolphinarium, and numerous cafes. The park is also home to the Varna Naval Museum, where visitors can explore naval history and see a range of maritime exhibits.

The nearby beaches, such as Golden Sands and Sunny Day, are perfect for sunbathing and swimming, with their fine sands and clear waters providing a quintessential Black Sea experience. These beaches are well-equipped with facilities and offer a range of water sports and relaxation options.

Cultural experiences in Varna include exploring the city's vibrant arts scene. The Varna Opera House frequently hosts performances ranging from classical to contemporary music, while the city's theaters and galleries offer a rich array of local and international art.

Dining in Varna is a treat for food lovers. For traditional Bulgarian cuisine, visit the Sasa Asian Cuisine, known for its delicious local dishes and warm atmosphere. For a more upscale dining experience, try the Restaurant at the Grand Hotel London, which offers a refined menu with a blend of Bulgarian and international flavors, accompanied by elegant service and stunning views.

Accommodation in Varna caters to all preferences. The Grand Hotel London provides luxurious accommodations in a historic building, offering a blend of old-world charm and modern amenities. For a more contemporary stay, the Hotel Golden Sands offers comfortable rooms with beautiful sea views and easy access to the beach. Budget travelers might prefer the Hotel Antik, which provides clean, affordable rooms with a central location.

Varna, with its rich blend of historical treasures, cultural experiences, and coastal charm, offers a memorable visit for travelers seeking both relaxation and exploration. Whether you're wandering through ancient ruins, enjoying the seaside, or indulging in local cuisine, Varna invites you to experience the diverse and vibrant spirit of Bulgaria's Black Sea coast.

Odessa, Ukraine

Odessa, Ukraine's lively port city on the Black Sea, offers a captivating blend of history, culture, and seaside charm. Known for its vibrant atmosphere and historic architecture, Odessa invites travelers to explore its rich heritage and enjoy its beautiful coastal setting.

Begin your exploration at the heart of Odessa, the Primorsky Boulevard. This picturesque promenade offers stunning views of the Black Sea and is lined with historic buildings, statues, and lively cafes. The iconic Potemkin Stairs, which descend from the boulevard to the harbor, are a must-see. These grand steps, made famous by Sergei Eisenstein's film "Battleship Potemkin," provide a dramatic entrance to the city and a fantastic photo opportunity.

Nearby, the Odessa Opera House stands as a testament to the city's cultural grandeur. This opulent building, with its ornate façade and stunning interior, hosts a variety of performances, including opera, ballet, and classical music. Catching a show here is a wonderful way to experience the local arts scene.

For a dose of local history, visit the Odessa Archaeological Museum. The museum's collection spans from ancient Greek and Roman artifacts to items from Ukraine's more recent history. Highlights include ancient coins, sculptures, and mummies, all offering insight into the region's past.

Outdoor enthusiasts will appreciate a visit to Odessa's beaches. Arcadia Beach, located just a short drive from the city center, is a popular spot for sunbathing and swimming. With its wide sandy shore and vibrant beach clubs, it's perfect for a day of relaxation. For a quieter experience, the more secluded beaches around the city provide a peaceful escape with fewer crowds.

The city's charming parks and gardens, such as Shevchenko Park, offer pleasant spots for leisurely walks and picnics. The park features beautifully landscaped gardens, fountains, and monuments, providing a serene environment away from the hustle and bustle of the city.

Odessa's cultural experiences extend to its bustling markets and street life. The Privoz Market is a vibrant place to experience local life, where vendors offer a wide range of fresh produce, meats, cheeses, and other goods. It's also a great place to sample local snacks and immerse yourself in the city's lively atmosphere.

Dining in Odessa is a delight, with options ranging from traditional Ukrainian fare to international cuisine. For authentic Ukrainian dishes, visit the Restaurant "Mushly" known for its delicious borscht, varenyky (dumplings), and hearty meat dishes. For a more contemporary dining experience, try "Nikolayevsky," which offers a diverse menu of both local and European dishes in a stylish setting. Seafood lovers should head to "Dacha" for fresh catches from the Black Sea, accompanied by stunning sea views.

Accommodation in Odessa ranges from luxury to budget-friendly options. The Hotel Bristol, located near the city center, offers elegant rooms and excellent service in a historic building. For a more modern stay, the M1 Club Hotel provides stylish accommodations with contemporary amenities and a prime location. Budget travelers can opt for the Deribas Hotel, which offers comfortable rooms and a central location at a more affordable price.

Odessa, with its dynamic mix of history, culture, and seaside allure, provides a rich and varied experience for visitors. From its historic landmarks and cultural institutions to its lively beaches and charming streets, the city invites travelers to explore its unique blend of past and present.

Sochi, Russia

Sochi, Russia's prominent resort city on the Black Sea, is renowned for its stunning coastal scenery and a rich mix of cultural and recreational experiences. With its subtropical climate, picturesque beaches, and modern amenities, Sochi has become a favored destination for both relaxation and exploration.

Begin your visit in the heart of Sochi at the Sochi Seaport. This bustling area serves as a major hub for maritime activities and offers pleasant promenades and a vibrant atmosphere. It's an ideal place for a leisurely stroll where you can take in the sea views and enjoy the lively ambiance.

A visit to Sochi's Central Beach is essential. Stretching along the city's coastline, this sandy beach provides ample opportunities for sunbathing and engaging in various water activities. The beach is lined with cafes and bars, making it a great spot to relax and enjoy the coastal charm.

For a touch of local history and culture, the Sochi History Museum is a must-see. Housed in a picturesque building, this museum offers insights into the city's development from ancient times through its modern evolution. The exhibits include artifacts, photographs, and documents that trace Sochi's transformation into a major resort destination.

The Sochi Arboretum, a sprawling botanical garden covering 49 hectares, is another highlight. This lush park is home to a diverse collection of plant species from around the world. Walking through the arboretum provides a peaceful escape and offers stunning views of the surrounding landscape and coastline.

Outdoor enthusiasts will appreciate the proximity of the Krasnaya Polyana mountains, which are easily accessible from Sochi. This area is well-known for its skiing and snowboarding opportunities in winter, as well as hiking and mountain biking during the summer months. The scenic beauty of the region, with its lush greenery and rugged terrain, makes it an ideal spot for outdoor activities.

For cultural experiences, the Winter Theatre stands out as a notable venue. This historic building hosts a range of performances, including ballets, operas, and concerts, providing a glimpse into Sochi's vibrant arts scene. Attending a performance here can be a memorable highlight of your visit.

When it comes to dining, Sochi offers a variety of options reflecting both local and international cuisines. Restoran Ogojda, situated near the beach, is popular for its seafood dishes and picturesque views. For a traditional Russian dining experience, Kavkazskaya Plennitsa serves hearty meals with an emphasis on regional specialties. If you're in the mood for international fare, Sakura offers a diverse menu with a focus on Asian cuisine.

Accommodation in Sochi caters to various preferences, from luxurious resorts to budget-friendly options. Rixos Krasnaya Polyana Sochi provides a high-end experience with stunning views, top-notch amenities, and easy access to nearby mountain activities. For a more central location with modern comforts, Marins Park Hotel is a good choice, offering convenient access to the city's attractions and waterfront. Budget travelers might consider Hotel Luzhniki, which offers comfortable rooms at a more affordable rate and is well-situated for exploring the city.

Sochi, with its blend of scenic beauty, cultural richness, and recreational opportunities, offers a well-rounded experience for travelers. Whether you're relaxing on the beach, exploring botanical gardens, or enjoying the local cuisine, Sochi promises an engaging and enjoyable visit.

CHAPTER 8.

ISLAND DESTINATION

The allure of island destinations lies in their enchanting isolation, breathtaking natural beauty, and the promise of unique, memorable experiences. Each island offers its own charm, from pristine beaches and crystal-clear waters to rich cultural tapestries and historic landmarks. Whether you're drawn to the vibrant vibrancy of tropical paradises or the serene seclusion of remote isles, island destinations provide a diverse array of experiences that captivate and inspire travelers.

Imagine arriving at an island and immediately being enveloped by a landscape of dazzling azure seas and verdant hills. The rhythm of the waves and the gentle sea breeze set a tranquil tone, inviting you to unwind and immerse yourself in the island's natural splendor. These destinations often feature some of the world's most stunning beaches, where powdery white sand meets turquoise waters, creating perfect spots for sunbathing, swimming, and water sports.

Beyond the beaches, islands frequently boast lush landscapes and diverse ecosystems. Tropical islands may be covered in dense rainforests or offer scenic hiking trails leading to breathtaking viewpoints. In contrast, temperate islands might feature rolling hills, charming vineyards, and serene lakes. Exploring these natural wonders provides opportunities for adventure and relaxation, whether you're hiking through a national park, snorkeling among vibrant coral reefs, or simply enjoying the view from a seaside cliff.

Island destinations are also rich in cultural heritage. Many islands have their own unique traditions, cuisines, and festivals that reflect their history and influences from various cultures. You might discover vibrant local markets where artisans showcase their crafts, or dine in charming restaurants offering regional specialties that highlight the island's culinary heritage. The blend of local customs and global influences creates a vibrant cultural mosaic that adds depth to your travel experience.

Historic sites and landmarks often add another layer of intrigue to island destinations. Ancient ruins, colonial architecture, and historical forts tell the stories of the islands' past, offering fascinating insights into their cultural evolution. These sites are not only educational but also provide picturesque settings that enhance the island's allure.

Accommodation on islands ranges from luxurious resorts and boutique hotels to cozy guesthouses and beachside bungalows. Each option offers its own level of comfort and style, ensuring that you can find a place that suits your preferences and budget. Many accommodations take full advantage of their natural surroundings, offering stunning views, private beach access, and personalized service that enhances your island experience.

Whether you seek relaxation, adventure, or cultural enrichment, island destinations cater to a wide range of interests. The combination of idyllic landscapes, unique cultural experiences, and luxurious or rustic accommodations makes each island a special place to explore and enjoy. As you set foot on these islands, you embark on a journey that promises to be as diverse and captivating as the destinations themselves.

Sardinia, Italy

Sardinia, Italy's second-largest island, is a dazzling gem in the Mediterranean, renowned for its stunning coastline, rugged mountains, and rich cultural heritage. This island offers a diverse array of experiences, from idyllic beaches and ancient ruins to charming villages and flavorful cuisine.

Begin your Sardinian adventure with a visit to the Costa Smeralda, the island's most famous stretch of coastline. Known for its turquoise waters and pristine white sandy beaches, this area is a paradise for beachgoers. The beaches of Porto Cervo and Porto Rotondo are particularly celebrated for their beauty and exclusive resorts. The crystal-clear waters are perfect for swimming, sunbathing, and water sports, while the surrounding area boasts luxurious boutiques and sophisticated dining options.

Explore the La Maddalena Archipelago, a group of islands off the northeastern coast of Sardinia. Accessible by ferry from Palau, these islands are renowned for their unspoiled natural beauty and are ideal for a day of island-hopping. The beaches of Spargi and Budelli are especially famous for their pink sand and azure waters, offering fantastic opportunities for snorkeling and relaxation.

For outdoor enthusiasts, the Gennargentu National Park in the heart of Sardinia presents a dramatic landscape of rugged mountains, deep gorges, and ancient forests. The park offers excellent hiking trails, such as the path to Punta La Marmora, the highest peak on the island, which provides panoramic views of the surrounding terrain. In addition to hiking, the park is great for bird-watching and exploring traditional Sardinian villages nestled in the mountains.

Cultural experiences abound in Sardinia, with its rich tapestry of history and tradition. The ancient ruins of Nora, located near Pula, offer a glimpse into Sardinia's Roman past with its well-preserved mosaics and theater. Another significant site is the Su Nuraxi of Barumini, a UNESCO World Heritage site that features a complex of prehistoric stone structures known as nuraghes. These ancient ruins are a testament to the island's early civilization and provide a fascinating insight into Sardinia's past.

The city of Cagliari, Sardinia's capital, is a vibrant destination with a blend of modern and historic elements. Wander through the Castello district, where narrow medieval streets and ancient walls surround charming cafes and boutiques. The Roman Amphitheater and the National Archaeological Museum are must-visit sites for those interested in history.

When it comes to dining, Sardinia offers a variety of local specialties. Try Su Furriadroxu in Cagliari for traditional Sardinian dishes, including roasted meats and rich stews. Ristorante Da Cesare in Porto Cervo is known for its seafood and stunning views of the harbor. For a taste of Sardinian pastries, don't miss Pasticceria Dessi in Alghero, where you can sample traditional sweets like sebadas and pani carasau.

Accommodation in Sardinia caters to various preferences and budgets. Luxurious options include the Hotel Cala di Volpe on the Costa Smeralda, which offers upscale amenities and breathtaking views. For a more intimate experience, Hotel La Villa in the town of Oristano provides charming rooms and a central location. Budget travelers might opt for Camping Village Torre del Porticciolo, which offers comfortable lodging and easy access to nearby beaches and outdoor activities.

Sardinia, with its captivating landscapes, rich cultural history, and warm hospitality, presents a destination that promises a diverse and fulfilling travel experience. Whether you're soaking up the sun on a pristine beach, exploring ancient ruins, or savoring local cuisine, Sardinia invites you to discover its unique charm and beauty.

Sicily, Italy

Sicily, the largest island in the Mediterranean Sea, is a place where ancient history, vibrant culture, and stunning landscapes converge. This Italian gem offers travelers a rich tapestry of experiences, from its dramatic coastline and volcanic landscapes to its historic cities and delectable cuisine.

Start your Sicilian adventure in Palermo, the island's bustling capital. The city is a melting pot of architectural styles and cultural influences. Wander through the lively markets, such as the Ballarò and Vucciria, where the vibrant atmosphere and colorful stalls offer a taste of local life. Visit the Palermo Cathedral, a stunning blend of Norman, Gothic, and Baroque styles, and don't miss the nearby Cappella Palatina, renowned for its dazzling mosaics.

A short drive from Palermo will take you to the ancient ruins of Segesta, where the well-preserved Doric temple and theater stand testament to the island's Greek past. Another must-see is the Valley of the Temples in Agrigento, an expansive archaeological site featuring some of the best-preserved ancient Greek temples outside Greece. The imposing Temple of Concordia and the Temple of Juno are highlights of this historical marvel.

For a glimpse of Sicily's volcanic landscape, head to Mount Etna, Europe's highest and most active volcano. A trip to Etna offers breathtaking views of the surrounding countryside and the opportunity to explore volcanic craters and lava fields. Hiking trails cater to various skill levels, and guided tours provide fascinating insights into the geology and history of this majestic mountain.

Sicily's outdoor offerings extend beyond its volcanic terrain. The island's coastline features some of the Mediterranean's most beautiful beaches. San Vito Lo Capo, with its crystal-clear waters and white sandy beach, is ideal for a day of sunbathing and swimming. For a more rugged coastal experience, the Scala dei Turchi near Realmonte boasts striking white limestone cliffs that rise dramatically from the sea.

Cultural enthusiasts will find much to explore in cities like Catania and Syracuse. Catania's historic center, with its baroque buildings and lively squares, reflects its rich history and vibrant culture. The Roman amphitheater and the Cathedral of Saint Agatha are key sites to visit. Syracuse, on the other hand, is home to the impressive archaeological park of Neapolis, featuring ancient Greek and Roman ruins, including a theater and an amphitheater. The island's rich history continues on Ortigia, the old town of Syracuse, with its charming streets and beautiful piazzas.

Sicilian cuisine is a highlight of any visit. In Palermo, sample street food like arancini (stuffed rice balls) and panelle (chickpea fritters) from local vendors. For a more sit-down experience, try Antica Focacceria San Francesco, a historic eatery serving traditional Sicilian dishes. In Catania, enjoy a meal at Trattoria da Antonio, known for its fresh seafood and local specialties. In Taormina, the restaurant La Capinera offers exquisite dining with a view of the sea.

Accommodation options in Sicily cater to various tastes and budgets. In Palermo, the Grand Hotel Wagner provides elegant rooms and a central location. For a more boutique experience, consider the Palazzo Brunaccini, with its charming decor and personalized service. In Taormina, the Belmond Grand Hotel Timeo offers luxurious amenities and stunning views of Mount Etna. Budget travelers might opt for Hotel Delle Palme in Palermo or the Hotel Villa Sonia in Castelmola, which offers comfortable lodging at a more affordable rate.

Cyprus

Cyprus, an enchanting island in the eastern Mediterranean, blends ancient history with vibrant modern life, offering travelers a rich tapestry of experiences. From sun-kissed beaches and majestic ruins to charming villages and culinary delights, Cyprus caters to every interest.

Begin your journey in Nicosia, the island's capital and its last divided city. Wander through the old town, known as the walled city, with its maze of narrow streets and historic architecture. The Cyprus Museum is a must-visit for history enthusiasts, housing an extensive collection of artifacts from the island's long history. Don't miss the Ledra Street Crossing Point, where you can walk between the Greek and Turkish sides of the city and gain insight into the island's complex history.

In the southern part of Cyprus, Limassol offers a blend of modern amenities and historic charm. Stroll along the vibrant Limassol Marina, a waterfront development with upscale shops, restaurants, and stunning views of the Mediterranean. The Limassol Castle, a medieval fortress, is another highlight, now housing the Cyprus Medieval Museum with exhibits on medieval Cypriot history.

Paphos, located on the western coast, is renowned for its archaeological treasures. The Paphos Archaeological Park is home to the well-preserved Paphos Mosaics, featuring intricate Roman floor mosaics depicting scenes from mythology. Nearby, the Tomb of the Kings provides a glimpse into ancient burial practices with its impressive underground tombs carved into the rock.

Outdoor enthusiasts will find plenty to explore. The Troodos Mountains, located in the island's interior, offer a scenic escape with opportunities for hiking, mountain biking, and exploring picturesque villages like Omodos and Platres. Aphrodite's Rock near Paphos is a natural landmark steeped in legend, said to be the birthplace of the goddess Aphrodite. It's a striking spot for a beach walk and photo opportunity.

Cyprus's coastline is dotted with beautiful beaches. Fig Tree Bay in Protaras is known for its golden sands and clear waters, making it ideal for swimming and sunbathing. For a more tranquil experience, visit Nissi Beach in Ayia Napa, famous for its soft sand and shallow waters, perfect for relaxation.

Cultural experiences on the island include exploring traditional villages like Lefkara, renowned for its lace and silverware. The village's quaint streets are lined with artisan shops and cafes where you can experience local crafts and hospitality. The Kykkos Monastery in the Troodos Mountains is another cultural gem, famous for its stunning frescoes and religious artifacts.

Cypriot cuisine is a delight for food lovers. In Nicosia, Mamas offers authentic Cypriot dishes in a charming setting. In Limassol, Meze Taverna serves a variety of traditional meze dishes, perfect for sampling a range of flavors. For a fine dining experience, The Grill Room in Nicosia provides an elegant atmosphere and a menu featuring both local and international dishes.

Accommodation options in Cyprus range from luxurious resorts to budget-friendly stays. The Anassa Hotel in Latchi offers a high-end experience with stunning sea views and top-notch amenities. For a boutique experience, Columbia Beach Resort in Pissouri combines charm with comfort and beautiful surroundings. Budget travelers might consider Hotel Nicosia in the capital or Elias Beach Hotel in Limassol, which provide good value and convenient locations.

Mallorca, Spain

Mallorca, the largest of Spain's Balearic Islands, is a Mediterranean paradise renowned for its stunning landscapes, rich history, and vibrant culture. With its dramatic coastlines, serene beaches, and charming towns, Mallorca offers a variety of experiences that cater to all types of travelers.

Start your exploration in Palma, the island's capital and a hub of cultural and architectural beauty. The city is dominated by the impressive Palma Cathedral, an architectural marvel that overlooks the harbor. Inside, you'll find a striking blend of Gothic and modernist elements, with the serene interior offering a peaceful escape from the bustling city outside. Nearby, the Royal Palace of La Almudaina provides a glimpse into Mallorca's regal past with its grand halls and scenic views of the city and harbor.

Venturing beyond Palma, the Serra de Tramuntana mountain range, a UNESCO World Heritage site, is a must-see. The range stretches along the island's northwest coast and offers breathtaking scenery with its rugged peaks and deep valleys. Hiking enthusiasts will enjoy trails such as the path to Castell d'Alaró, which rewards with panoramic views of the island. The picturesque village of Valldemossa nestled in the mountains is famous for its charming streets and the historic charterhouse where Chopin spent a winter.

For a taste of Mallorca's coastal charm, visit the beautiful beaches of Cala Millor and Cala d'Or. Cala Millor, with its long stretch of golden sand and clear waters, is ideal for sunbathing and swimming. Cala d'Or, known for its series of small, sheltered coves, offers a more intimate beach experience with excellent opportunities for snorkeling.

Outdoor adventures abound on the island. The Sierra de Tramuntana offers excellent hiking, mountain biking, and rock climbing opportunities. For a unique experience, explore the Caves of Drach near Porto Cristo. These impressive limestone caves feature underground lakes and stunning stalactite formations. A boat ride across the subterranean lake is a memorable way to experience the natural beauty of the caves.

Mallorca's cultural experiences are rich and varied. The Museu de Mallorca in Palma provides insights into the island's history and art through its extensive collection of artifacts and artworks. In the town of Inca, renowned for its leather goods, the local market offers an authentic glimpse into traditional Mallorcan life and craftsmanship. Additionally, the annual Festa de Sant Joan in Palma celebrates with vibrant parades, fireworks, and traditional music.

When it comes to dining, Mallorca boasts a wide range of options from casual tapas bars to fine dining establishments. Café Ricasoli in Palma is a great place to enjoy traditional Mallorcan dishes such as pa amb oli and sobrasada. For a fine dining experience, Marc Fosh offers a sophisticated menu with a focus on contemporary Mediterranean cuisine. Es Verger, located in the mountains near Alaró, is famed for its roast lamb and rustic charm.

Accommodation on the island ranges from luxurious resorts to cozy boutique hotels. The Belmond La Residencia in Deià offers an upscale experience with elegant rooms, beautiful gardens, and stunning views of the surrounding mountains. For a more central location, the Hotel Astoria Playa in Palma provides modern comforts and easy access to the city's attractions. Budget travelers might consider Hostel A2B in Palma for a comfortable and affordable stay close to the city center.

Mallorca, with its blend of natural beauty, cultural richness, and welcoming atmosphere, offers a captivating destination for travelers.

Corsica, France

Corsica, a striking island in the Mediterranean Sea, is a treasure trove of rugged landscapes, pristine beaches, and vibrant culture. Known for its dramatic coastlines, mountainous terrain, and historical charm, Corsica offers a wealth of experiences for travelers seeking both adventure and relaxation.

Begin your journey in Ajaccio, the island's capital and the birthplace of Napoleon Bonaparte. Ajaccio boasts a charming old town with narrow streets and a picturesque harbor. Maison Bonaparte, Napoleon's ancestral home, provides fascinating insights into his early life and Corsican heritage. The Ajaccio Cathedral, with its distinctive pink facade, is also worth a visit, offering a glimpse into local religious architecture and history.

Traveling north, Bastia presents a different side of Corsica. This bustling port city is known for its lively atmosphere and historic sites. The Old Port area is lined with cafes and shops, perfect for a leisurely stroll. The Citadel of Bastia offers panoramic views of the city and the surrounding coastline, and the Church of Saint John the Baptist is notable for its elegant baroque interior.

For natural beauty and outdoor activities, head to the Scandola Nature Reserve, a UNESCO World Heritage site accessible only by boat. The reserve is renowned for its dramatic cliffs, crystal-clear waters, and unique rock formations. Boat tours provide an exceptional vantage point to appreciate the reserve's rugged beauty and diverse marine life.

Corte, located in the heart of Corsica, is a must-visit for those interested in the island's mountainous terrain and history. The town is home to the Musée de la Corse, which delves into Corsican culture and history. The nearby Restonica Valley offers breathtaking hiking opportunities with trails leading through lush forests and to picturesque mountain lakes.

Corsica's coastline is dotted with stunning beaches. Palombaggia Beach near Porto-Vecchio is famous for its white sand and turquoise waters, ideal for sunbathing and swimming. Rondinara Beach, located between Porto-Vecchio and Bonifacio, is known for its crescent-shaped bay and clear, shallow waters perfect for families.

For cultural immersion, explore the charming village of Bonifacio, perched on limestone cliffs overlooking the sea. The town is known for its historic fortifications, narrow streets, and stunning sea views. The Bonifacio Citadel and the Escalier du Roi d'Aragon, a dramatic staircase carved into the cliffside, are highlights.

Corsican cuisine reflects a blend of French and Italian influences with a distinctive local twist. Try Chez Paul in Ajaccio for traditional Corsican dishes such as wild boar stew and local cheeses. In Porto-Vecchio, La Table de la Ferme offers a farm-to-table dining experience with a focus on fresh, local ingredients. For a taste of Corsican pastries, Patisserie Mela in Bastia is renowned for its sweet treats.

Accommodation in Corsica ranges from luxurious resorts to charming guesthouses. Hotel La Pinède in Porto-Vecchio offers upscale amenities with stunning views of the surrounding beaches. Le Domaine de Murtoli, located in the southern part of the island, provides a unique blend of luxury and traditional Corsican charm, set in a picturesque rural setting. For more budget-conscious travelers, Hotel Fesch in Ajaccio offers comfortable rooms and a central location, making it a convenient base for exploring the city.

Corsica, with its rugged landscapes, rich history, and vibrant culture, provides a multifaceted destination for travelers. Whether exploring ancient towns, relaxing on beautiful beaches, or hiking through majestic mountains, the island offers a range of experiences that highlight its unique and captivating charm.

CHAPTER 9

EXCURSIONS AND DAY TRIPS

Guided Tours vs. Independent Exploration

When visiting Mediterranean ports, one of the key decisions you'll face is whether to join a guided tour or explore independently. Each option has its pros and cons, depending on your travel style, budget, and interests. Here's a detailed guide to help you decide what's best for your Mediterranean cruise experience.

1. Guided Tours

Guided tours are organized excursions led by local experts or professional guides who take you through the key attractions, offering historical context, cultural insights, and logistical convenience.

- Pros of Guided Tours:
    - Expert Knowledge: A major benefit of guided tours is access to knowledgeable guides who can provide in-depth information about the sites you're visiting. They often share historical facts, interesting anecdotes, and cultural insights that you might miss on your own.
    - Hassle-Free Experience: For Guided tours, they take care of all the details, from transportation to entrance fees, allowing you to relax and enjoy the experience. This is particularly advantageous in busy or unfamiliar

locations where navigating on your own might be challenging.

- Priority Access: Many guided tours offer skip-the-line privileges at popular attractions, saving you time and allowing you to see more in a limited timeframe. This can be especially useful at major sites like the Vatican in Rome or the Sagrada Familia in Barcelona, where lines can be long.

- Safety and Security: Traveling in a group with a guide provides an added layer of security, especially in unfamiliar areas. Guides are also familiar with the local customs and can help you avoid potential pitfalls.

- Social Interaction: If you enjoy meeting other travelers, guided tours can be a great way to connect with like-minded people. Group tours often include travelers from around the world, creating opportunities for social interaction and shared experiences.

- Cons of Guided Tours:

- Less Flexibility: Guided tours follow a fixed itinerary, which means you'll have less flexibility to explore at your own pace or spend extra time at places that interest you. This can be limiting if you prefer a more spontaneous travel experience.

- Crowds and Group Dynamics: Some guided tours can be crowded, especially during peak tourist seasons. Being part of a large group might mean waiting for others and moving at a slower pace than you'd prefer. Additionally, group dynamics can sometimes affect your enjoyment, depending on the mix of personalities.

- Cost: Guided tours can be more expensive than exploring independently, especially if you opt for private or small-group tours. While they often provide value in terms of convenience and knowledge, the cost might not fit everyone's budget.

2. Independent Exploration

Independent exploration allows you to discover a destination at your own convenience, without the constraints of a group or guide. This option is ideal for travelers who value freedom, flexibility, and the thrill of discovering a place on their own.

- Pros of Independent Exploration:
  - Complete Flexibility: When you explore independently, you have the freedom to create your own itinerary, linger at places that capture your interest, and skip those that don't. You can also choose to explore lesser-known areas that might not be included in typical guided tours.
  - Personalized Experience: Independent travel allows you to tailor your day to your own interests and preferences. Whether you want to spend the morning at a museum, the afternoon shopping, or simply relax at a café, the choice is entirely yours.
  - Cost-Effective: Independent exploration can be more budget-friendly, as you have control over how much you spend on transportation, meals, and entrance fees. You can also opt for free or low-cost attractions, use public transportation, and find local eateries that fit your budget.
  - Immersive Experience: Exploring on your own can lead to a more immersive experience, as you interact with locals, navigate public transport, and discover hidden gems off the beaten path. It's a great way to get a deeper sense of the local culture and way of life.

- Privacy: Independent exploration offers the advantage of privacy and personal space. Whether you're traveling solo or with a companion, you can enjoy the experience without the dynamics of a larger group.

- Cons of Independent Exploration:
  - Time-Consuming Planning: Independent exploration requires more planning and research, as you'll need to figure out transportation, navigate maps, and decide on the best places to visit. This can be time-consuming and requires a good level of organization.
  - Language Barriers: In some Mediterranean ports, language barriers can be a challenge. While many people in tourist areas speak English, having some basic knowledge of the local language or using translation apps can be helpful.
  - Logistical Challenges: Navigating a new city on your own can sometimes be challenging, especially in larger cities or more complex destinations. You might miss out on certain highlights if you're not familiar with the area or if transportation options are limited.
  - Limited Historical and Cultural Context: Without a guide, you might miss out on detailed historical and cultural information. While guidebooks and audio guides can help fill in the gaps, they may not offer the same level of depth and insight as a knowledgeable local guide.
  - Safety Concerns: Traveling independently requires a heightened awareness of your surroundings, particularly in busy tourist areas where pickpocketing can be an issue. It's important to stay vigilant and take precautions to ensure your safety.

Making the Decision

- Assess Your Priorities: Think about what you want to get out of your day at each port. If you value in-depth knowledge, convenience, and the security of a group, a guided tour might be the better option. If you prefer flexibility, independence, and a more personalized experience, consider exploring on your own.

- Consider the Destination: Some ports are easier to navigate independently than others. For example, in cities with well-developed public transportation systems, like Barcelona or Nice, independent exploration can be straightforward. In contrast, more remote or sprawling destinations, like the Ephesus, Turkey might be better suited to guided tours.

- Budget and Time: Guided tours can be more expensive, but they also save you time and can offer better access to certain attractions. If you're on a tight schedule or have specific sights you don't want to miss, a guided tour might be worth the investment. On the other hand, if you have more time and prefer a leisurely pace, exploring independently could be more rewarding.

- Blend Both Options: Many travelers find a mix of guided tours and independent exploration works best. For example, you might choose a guided tour for a complex destination or historical site and explore other ports on your own. This approach gives you the best of both worlds, allowing you to enjoy the benefits of guided experiences while also having the freedom to wander and discover at your own pace.

In summary, whether you choose a guided tour or go it alone, both options offer unique advantages that can enhance your Mediterranean cruise experience. Consider your preferences, the destination, and your budget to make the best decision for each port you visit. Ultimately, the goal is to enjoy the rich history, culture, and beauty of the Mediterranean in a way that suits your travel style.

Top day trips from key ports

When cruising through the Mediterranean, you have the chance to explore more than just the port cities. Day trips offer a perfect opportunity to immerse yourself in the region's rich history, stunning landscapes, and vibrant cultures. Here's a guide to some of the top day trips from key Mediterranean ports, providing everything you need to know to make the most of these excursions.

Barcelona, Spain: Montserrat

Just an hour from Barcelona, Montserrat is a remarkable day trip destination renowned for its unique mountain formations and historic monastery. The journey to Montserrat is scenic, often involving a train ride followed by a cable car or funicular to the top. Once there, you can visit the Santa Maria de Montserrat Abbey, home to the revered Black Madonna. The abbey offers panoramic views of the surrounding landscape, making it a great spot for photography. For those interested in hiking, Montserrat features various trails that provide stunning views and a chance to experience the natural beauty of the area. Many guided tours from Barcelona include transportation and a local guide to enrich your visit with historical and cultural insights.

Marseille, France: Aix-en-Provence

A short drive from Marseille, Aix-en-Provence is a charming town known for its beautiful architecture and vibrant markets. The town's highlights include Cézanne's Studio, where the famous painter created many of his masterpieces. Strolling down Cours Mirabeau, a lively street lined with cafes and shops, you'll experience the local atmosphere and find opportunities for shopping and dining. The Saint-Sauveur Cathedral, with its blend of architectural styles, is another must-see. You can reach Aix-en-Provence by train or shuttle bus from Marseille, and guided tours often provide convenient transportation and a detailed exploration of the town's main attractions.

Nice, France: Monaco

Monaco, the glamorous city-state just a short train ride from Nice, is known for its luxury and elegance. The Monte Carlo Casino is a highlight, where you can admire its opulent architecture and try your luck at the gaming tables. The Prince's Palace offers a glimpse into the royal history of Monaco, and you can catch the changing of the guard ceremony. The old town, Monaco-Ville, is perfect for exploring narrow streets, historic buildings, and stunning views. Regular train services make it easy to travel between Nice and Monaco, and many cruise lines offer excursions that include transportation and guided tours to help you navigate this dazzling destination.

Civitavecchia (Rome), Italy: Rome

Rome, the capital of Italy, is a treasure trove of historical and cultural landmarks. A day trip to Rome from Civitavecchia is a chance to explore iconic sites such as the Colosseum, where you can delve into the history of ancient gladiatorial games. Vatican City, home to St. Peter's Basilica, the Vatican Museums, and the Sistine Chapel, offers a profound cultural experience. The Roman Forum, with its ancient ruins, provides insight into the daily life of ancient Romans. Civitavecchia is about an hour and a half from Rome by train or car, and many excursions include guided tours and transportation, ensuring you make the most of your visit to this historic city.

Naples, Italy: Pompeii

The ancient city of Pompeii, buried by the eruption of Mount Vesuvius in AD 79, offers a fascinating glimpse into Roman life. A day trip from Naples allows you to explore the well-preserved ruins, including homes, temples, and the amphitheater. You can also visit Mount Vesuvius and hike to the crater for panoramic views of the surrounding area. The Pompeii Archaeological Museum provides additional context with artifacts from the site. Pompeii is about a 30-minute drive from Naples, and many tours include transportation and a guided walk through the ruins, enhancing your understanding of this remarkable archaeological site.

Dubrovnik, Croatia: Montenegro's Bay of Kotor

The Bay of Kotor, with its dramatic fjord-like landscape and medieval towns, is a stunning destination accessible from Dubrovnik. In Kotor, explore the UNESCO-listed old town, climb the city walls for breathtaking views, and discover the historic churches and squares. Perast, a charming town nearby, offers boat trips to Our Lady of the Rocks island. Budva, known for its beaches and lively nightlife, is another highlight. The Bay of Kotor is about a 2-hour drive from Dubrovnik, and many excursions offer guided tours and transportation, allowing you to fully appreciate the beauty and history of this picturesque region.

Athens (Piraeus), Greece: Delphi

Delphi, an important ancient Greek religious site, is located about 2.5 hours from Athens. A day trip to Delphi includes exploring the archaeological site, where you can see the Temple of Apollo, the ancient theater, and the Sanctuary of Athena. The Delphi Archaeological Museum houses significant artifacts, including the famous Charioteer of Delphi statue. The mountainous scenery around Delphi adds to the experience, providing stunning views of the valley below. Delphi is reachable by car or bus from Athens, and guided tours often include transportation and expert commentary on the site's historical significance.

Istanbul, Turkey: Ephesus

Ephesus, with its ancient ruins and historical significance, is a must-visit destination from Istanbul. The Library of Celsus, the Great Theatre, and the Temple of Artemis are among the highlights of this well-preserved city. The ruins offer a glimpse into the grandeur of Roman architecture and urban planning. Ephesus is about an hour's drive from Kusadasi, a common port for cruises in the region. Many tours include transportation and a guide, ensuring a comprehensive exploration of the site and its historical context.

These day trips provide a rich and varied experience of the Mediterranean region, offering opportunities to delve deeper into its history, culture, and natural beauty. Whether you choose guided tours for convenience and insight or explore independently for a more personal adventure, each destination promises memorable experiences and unique discoveries.

Historical Excursions

Exploring historical sites during your Mediterranean cruise provides a window into the region's rich past. From ancient ruins to medieval fortresses, these excursions offer a chance to immerse yourself in history and understand the cultural heritage of the Mediterranean. Here's a guide to some notable historical excursions from key Mediterranean ports, highlighting what to expect and what you need to know.

1. Rome (Civitavecchia), Italy: Ancient Rome and Vatican City

A day trip from Civitavecchia to Rome is a deep dive into ancient history. Start with a visit to the Colosseum, the iconic amphitheater where gladiatorial games were once held. Guided tours typically include access to the arena floor, underground chambers, and the upper tiers, providing insight into its construction and use.

Next, explore the Roman Forum, the heart of ancient Rome's political, social, and economic life. Wander through the ruins of temples, basilicas, and public spaces that once bustled with activity. The nearby Palatine Hill offers panoramic views of the Forum and is steeped in Roman legend as the birthplace of Rome.

A visit to Vatican City is a must. Tour the Vatican Museums, which house an extensive collection of art and historical artifacts, culminating in the Sistine Chapel with Michelangelo's famous ceiling frescoes. Don't miss St. Peter's Basilica, a masterpiece of Renaissance architecture. Many excursions from Civitavecchia offer guided tours of these sites, providing historical context and ensuring a thorough visit.

2. Athens (Piraeus), Greece: The Acropolis

From Piraeus, a short trip leads you to Athens, where the Acropolis stands as a symbol of ancient Greek civilization. The Acropolis Museum provides an introduction to the site, showcasing artifacts and sculptures found on the hill.

On the Acropolis itself, explore the Parthenon, a temple dedicated to the goddess Athena, which exemplifies classical Greek architecture. The Erechtheion, with its iconic Caryatids, and the Temple of Athena Nike are also notable structures. Guided tours often include insights into the mythology, history, and architectural significance of these ancient buildings.

For a comprehensive experience, consider combining your Acropolis visit with a tour of ancient Agora, the marketplace and civic center of Athens, where you can see well-preserved ruins of temples, the Stoa of Attalos, and the Temple of Hephaestus.

3. Ephesus (Kusadasi), Turkey: Ancient Ephesus

Ephesus, reachable from Kusadasi, is one of the best-preserved ancient cities in the Mediterranean. Begin your exploration at the Library of Celsus, an impressive structure that once housed thousands of scrolls. Nearby, the Great Theatre, with a seating capacity of up to 25,000, is still used for performances today.

Walk along Marble Street, lined with columns and remnants of once-grand buildings, and visit the Temple of Artemis, one of the Seven Wonders of the Ancient World. The Terrace Houses, featuring well-preserved mosaics and frescoes, offer a glimpse into the lives of Ephesus's wealthy residents. Guided tours often provide historical context and detailed explanations of these fascinating ruins.

4. Pompeii (Naples), Italy: The Ruins of Pompeii

A visit to Pompeii, accessible from Naples, is like stepping back in time. The ancient city was buried by Mount Vesuvius's eruption in 79 AD, preserving it in a unique state. Explore the remarkably preserved streets, houses, and public buildings, including the Forum, the Basilica, and the amphitheater.

Tour guides typically explain the daily life of Pompeii's residents, the eruption's impact, and the city's discovery and excavation. Visit the Villa of the Mysteries to see well-preserved frescoes that offer insights into ancient Roman art and rituals.

Consider combining your Pompeii visit with a trip to Mount Vesuvius itself. Many excursions offer a hike to the crater's edge, where you can enjoy stunning views of the Bay of Naples and the surrounding countryside.

5. Dubrovnik, Croatia: The Old Town

Dubrovnik, known for its well-preserved medieval architecture, offers a historical excursion through its

UNESCO-listed Old Town. Walk along the city walls, which provide panoramic views of the Adriatic Sea and the terracotta rooftops of the old city. The walls are an excellent example of defensive architecture from the medieval period.

Within the Old Town, explore historic landmarks such as the Rector's Palace, which once served as the seat of government, and the Franciscan Monastery, which houses one of the oldest pharmacies in Europe. The Sponza Palace, with its Renaissance architecture, is another highlight. Guided tours often include rich historical narratives about Dubrovnik's role in trade, politics, and culture during the Middle Ages.

6. Valletta, Malta: The Historic City of Valletta

Valletta, Malta's capital, is a treasure trove of history. The city, founded by the Knights of St. John, is known for its Baroque architecture and fortifications. Visit St. John's Co-Cathedral to admire its ornate interior and the famous Caravaggio painting, "The Beheading of Saint John the Baptist."

Explore the Grand Master's Palace, which served as the residence of the Knights and now houses the Parliament. Walk through the Upper Barracca Gardens for a panoramic view of the Grand Harbour. Guided tours often include historical insights into Valletta's strategic importance and the Knights' influence on its development.

CHAPTER 10

LOCAL CUISINE AND DINING EXPERIENCES

Mediterranean Food Highlights

The Mediterranean region is renowned for its vibrant and diverse culinary traditions, reflecting the rich cultural tapestry of the area. From the sun-drenched coasts of Spain to the aromatic markets of Turkey, each country along the Mediterranean has its unique flavors and ingredients. Here's a detailed guide to the must-try dishes at each key port.

1. Barcelona, Spain
Must-Try Dish: Paella
Barcelona, located in the Catalonia region, offers a unique twist on traditional Spanish paella. While Valencia is the birthplace of this dish, Barcelona's seaside location ensures that the paella de mariscos (seafood paella) is as fresh as it gets. Made with a rich blend of saffron-infused rice, prawns, mussels, and squid, this dish is cooked in a large, shallow pan to create a delightful crust at the bottom, known as socarrat.

Many restaurants serve paella as a shared dish, typically for two or more people. It's usually prepared fresh, so be prepared to wait around 20-30 minutes. Enjoy it with a glass of Cava, Catalonia's signature sparkling wine, for a true local experience.

2. Marseille, France

Have a taste of; Bouillabaisse

Marseille is famous for its bouillabaisse, a traditional Provençal fish stew that originated from this vibrant port city. This dish includes a variety of fish, such as red mullet, scorpionfish, and conger, along with shellfish like mussels and crab. The broth, infused with garlic, saffron, and fennel, is rich and aromatic, often served with rouille (a garlic and saffron mayonnaise) and crusty bread.

Bouillabaisse is typically served as a two-course meal—first, the broth is served, followed by the fish and shellfish. Look for restaurants that adhere to this tradition, as it indicates authenticity. A glass of Bandol rosé pairs perfectly with this dish.

3. Nice, France

Try out: Salade Niçoise

In the heart of the French Riviera, Nice offers the quintessential Salade Niçoise. This vibrant salad combines fresh tomatoes, hard-boiled eggs, Niçoise olives, anchovies, and tuna, all drizzled with olive oil and often served with a crisp baguette. It's a light yet satisfying dish, perfect for the warm Mediterranean climate.

Authentic Salade Niçoise is not served with cooked vegetables like green beans or potatoes, despite what you might find in some restaurants. For a local experience, enjoy this salad at an open-air café in the Old Town (Vieux Nice) with a glass of chilled rosé.

4. Rome, Italy
Must-Try Dish: Cacio e Pepe
Rome is the place to indulge in Cacio e Pepe, a deceptively simple pasta dish made with just three ingredients: pasta, Pecorino Romano cheese, and black pepper. The dish is a celebration of the quality of ingredients, with the creamy sauce created purely from the cheese and pasta water.

While it's tempting to add more, the beauty of Cacio e Pepe lies in its simplicity. Seek out a traditional trattoria in Trastevere or near the Pantheon for an authentic experience. Pair it with a glass of Frascati, a white wine from the Lazio region.

5. Naples, Italy
Dish: Pizza Margherita
Naples is the birthplace of pizza, and no trip to this port city is complete without trying the classic Pizza Margherita. This pizza, topped with San Marzano tomatoes, mozzarella di bufala, fresh basil, and a drizzle of extra-virgin olive oil, is a perfect example of how simple ingredients can create something extraordinary.

Neapolitan pizza is known for its soft, slightly chewy crust, cooked quickly in a wood-fired oven at high temperatures. For the best experience, visit a traditional pizzeria like L'Antica Pizzeria da Michele. Enjoy it with a cold Peroni beer or a glass of local Aglianico wine.

6. Athens, Greece
Dish: Moussaka

In Athens, moussaka is the dish to try. This hearty casserole layers eggplant, ground lamb, and béchamel sauce, baked to golden perfection. The flavors are rich and comforting, making it a staple of Greek cuisine.

Moussaka is best enjoyed at a traditional taverna. Look for spots frequented by locals rather than touristy areas for a more authentic experience. Pair it with a glass of Retsina, a Greek white wine flavored with pine resin, for a traditional accompaniment.

7. Istanbul, Turkey
Try; Kebabs
Istanbul offers a wide variety of kebabs, but the Adana kebab is particularly famous. Made from ground lamb, mixed with hot spices, and grilled on a skewer, this dish is both flavorful and filling. It's usually served with rice, grilled vegetables, and fresh pita bread.

For an authentic experience, visit a meyhane (Turkish tavern), where you can enjoy kebabs alongside a selection of meze and a glass of rakı (an anise-flavored spirit). Kebabs are often part of a larger meal, so come hungry and ready to sample several dishes.

8. Santorini, Greece
Dish: Fava
Santorini's volcanic soil produces some unique flavors, and fava is one of the island's signature dishes. This smooth, creamy dip is made from yellow split peas and is typically served with a drizzle of olive oil, capers, and sometimes caramelized onions.

Fava is often served as a starter, but it's filling enough to be enjoyed on its own with some fresh bread. Pair it with a glass of Assyrtiko, a crisp white wine native to Santorini, for a true taste of the island.

9. Palermo, Sicily
Must-Try Dish: Arancini
In Palermo, Sicily, arancini are a must-try. These deep-fried rice balls are stuffed with a variety of fillings, such as meat ragù, peas, and mozzarella, then coated in breadcrumbs and fried to golden perfection. They're crispy on the outside and soft and savory on the inside.

Arancini are often sold as street food, making them perfect for a quick snack while exploring the city. Pair them with a refreshing granita (a semi-frozen dessert) to balance the richness of the arancini.

10. Dubrovnik, Croatia

Try out: Black Risotto
Dubrovnik, located on the Adriatic coast, is known for its seafood, and black risotto (crni rižot) is a standout dish. This risotto gets its distinctive color from squid ink and is cooked with cuttlefish or squid, garlic, red wine, and olive oil, resulting in a rich, savory flavor.

Black risotto can be quite filling, so consider sharing if you're planning to try other local dishes. It pairs well with a glass of Malvazija wine, a dry white wine from the Istria region.

11. Valencia, Spain

Must-Try Dish: Horchata and Fartons

While in Valencia, don't miss trying horchata, a refreshing drink made from ground chufa (tiger nuts), water, and sugar. It's typically enjoyed with fartons, elongated, sweet pastries that are perfect for dipping into the horchata.

Horchata is best enjoyed cold, especially during the warm months. Visit a local horchatería for the freshest experience, and be sure to enjoy it as an afternoon snack.

Each Mediterranean port offers a culinary experience that's deeply rooted in its local culture and history. Whether you're savoring a classic pizza in Naples or indulging in fava on Santorini, these dishes are more than just food—they're a way to connect with the traditions and people of each destination. So, take your time, explore the local flavors, and let your taste buds guide you through the Mediterranean.

CHAPTER 11

ITINERARIES

7-Day Western Mediterranean Cruise Itinerary

A 7-day Western Mediterranean cruise is an ideal way to explore some of the most stunning and culturally rich ports in Europe. This itinerary is designed to give you a well-rounded experience, balancing iconic landmarks, local culture, and relaxation. Below is a day-by-day breakdown of what to expect, along with tips to help you make the most of your journey.

Day 1: Departure from Barcelona, Spain

Morning:
Your cruise begins in the vibrant city of Barcelona. Arrive a day early if possible to explore the city's highlights. Visit the Sagrada Família, Gaudí's unfinished masterpiece, or take a stroll down La Rambla. Before boarding, savor a leisurely lunch of tapas at a local bar, and perhaps a glass of Cava, a Catalan sparkling wine.

Afternoon:
Board your ship in the early afternoon. After settling into your cabin, explore the vessel's amenities. Attend the mandatory safety drill and then head to the deck for departure, watching the cityscape of Barcelona fade into the horizon.

Evening:
Enjoy your first dinner on board. Many cruise lines offer a welcome show or party, so take advantage of the entertainment and begin meeting fellow travelers.

Day 2: Marseille, France

Morning:
Your first port of call is Marseille, France's oldest city. Start your day with a visit to Le Vieux Port (The Old Port), where you can watch the fishermen unload their catch of the day. From there, head to Notre-Dame de la Garde, a basilica offering panoramic views of the city and coastline.

Afternoon:
After lunch, either on board or at a local café, explore Le Panier, Marseille's oldest district, with its narrow streets, artisan shops, and historic sites. Alternatively, you might opt for a guided tour to the nearby Calanques, stunning rocky inlets with turquoise waters, perfect for a quick swim or boat ride.

Evening:
Return to the ship in time for a relaxing dinner. As you sail away from Marseille, reflect on the city's mix of ancient and modern influences.

Day 3: Nice (Villefranche-sur-Mer), France

Morning:
Arrive in the charming port of Villefranche-sur-Mer, just a short distance from Nice. Take a scenic drive along the Promenade des Anglais in Nice, stopping at the Flower Market in Cours Saleya to admire the vibrant stalls filled with fresh produce, flowers, and local goods.

Afternoon:
Enjoy a leisurely lunch at a beachside restaurant, trying local dishes like Salade Niçoise. Spend the afternoon exploring Old Nice (Vieux Nice), with its narrow, winding streets, colorful buildings, and inviting shops. If you prefer something more adventurous, consider a trip to Monaco, just a short train ride away.

Evening:
Back on board, take in the sunset over the French Riviera. Tonight might be a good night to try one of the ship's specialty dining restaurants for a more intimate experience.

Day 4: Livorno (Florence/Pisa), Italy

Morning:
Dock at Livorno, your gateway to Tuscany. If this is your first visit, a day trip to Florence is a must. Start early with a visit to the Uffizi Gallery or the Accademia Gallery to see Michelangelo's David. Wander through the historic city center, visiting the Duomo and Piazza della Signoria.

Afternoon:

Have lunch at a traditional trattoria, savoring Tuscan specialties like ribollita or bistecca alla fiorentina. In the afternoon, head to Pisa to see the iconic Leaning Tower and explore the nearby Piazza dei Miracoli.

Evening:
Return to the ship in time for a late dinner. Enjoy a nightcap on deck as you sail towards your next destination, reflecting on the artistic and architectural wonders of the day.

Day 5: Civitavecchia (Rome), Italy

Morning:
Arrive in Civitavecchia, the port for Rome. Opt for an early start with a guided tour to make the most of your time. Begin with a visit to the Vatican Museums, including the Sistine Chapel and St. Peter's Basilica.

Afternoon:
After a quick lunch, continue your exploration with a visit to the Colosseum and the Roman Forum. Alternatively, you might choose to explore the Pantheon and Piazza Navona, or simply wander through the picturesque streets of Trastevere.

Evening:
Head back to Civitavecchia for an evening departure. As the ship leaves port, enjoy a traditional Italian dinner on board, perhaps accompanied by a fine glass of Italian wine.

Day 6: Naples (Pompeii/Amalfi Coast), Italy

Morning:
Dock in Naples, a city rich with history and culture. Start your day with a visit to Pompeii, the ancient city preserved by the eruption of Mount Vesuvius. Wander through the well-preserved ruins, imagining life as it was nearly 2,000 years ago.

Afternoon:
In the afternoon, choose between exploring Naples itself, with a stop at the National Archaeological Museum and sampling the city's famous pizza, or taking a scenic drive along the Amalfi Coast. Towns like Positano and Amalfi offer breathtaking views, charming shops, and delightful cafés.

Evening:
Return to the ship for your final evening at sea. Take time to relax, perhaps with a spa treatment or a quiet dinner, as you sail towards your final destination.

Final Day(7) Return to Barcelona, Spain

Late Morning:
If you have a few hours before your flight, use this time to explore a lesser-known side of Barcelona. Consider visiting the Poble Espanyol, an open-air museum that showcases the architectural styles and traditions from various regions of Spain. It's a peaceful way to spend your last few hours and pick up any final souvenirs.

Alternative Option:

For those who love art, the Picasso Museum is another excellent choice. Located in the Gothic Quarter, it houses an extensive collection of Pablo Picasso's works, giving you insight into the evolution of this iconic artist. The surrounding narrow streets are also perfect for one last leisurely stroll through Barcelona's historical heart.

Lunch:
Before heading to the airport, enjoy a final meal at one of Barcelona's traditional tapas bars. This is your last chance to indulge in local favorites like patatas bravas, jamón ibérico, and pan con tomate. If time permits, a quick stop at La Boqueria Market can offer a final taste of Catalonia's vibrant food scene.

Afternoon:
Return to the ship to collect your luggage if you left it on board, and then make your way to the airport. Barcelona's El Prat Airport is well-connected to the city center by taxi, bus, or train, making your departure as smooth as possible.

Evening:
As you board your flight, take a moment to reflect on the incredible journey you've just experienced. The Western Mediterranean has offered you a rich tapestry of cultures, histories, and landscapes, each port bringing its own unique flavor to your adventure.

As your Western Mediterranean cruise comes to an end, you'll likely find yourself filled with a deep appreciation for the diverse cultures and stunning vistas you've encountered.

10-Day Eastern Mediterranean Cruise Itinerary

Day 1: Departure from Venice, Italy

Morning: Embarkation
Your journey begins in the romantic city of Venice, where you'll board your cruise ship. Take some time to explore the ship and get familiar with your home for the next ten days.

Afternoon: Exploring Venice
Before setting sail, take advantage of your time in Venice. Explore the iconic St. Mark's Square, visit the Doge's Palace, and take a gondola ride along the Grand Canal. If time allows, lose yourself in the narrow alleyways and discover hidden gems like Campo Santa Margherita or the Jewish Ghetto.

Evening: Departure
As the ship sets sail in the early evening, head to the upper deck to enjoy breathtaking views of Venice fading into the distance. Relax with a welcome cocktail as you watch the sunset over the Adriatic Sea.

Day 2: Dubrovnik, Croatia

Morning: Arrival and Old Town Exploration
Wake up to the sight of the stunning walled city of Dubrovnik. Dubrovnik's Old Town is a UNESCO World Heritage site. Start your day by walking the ancient city walls for panoramic views of the city and the sea. Explore

the Stradun (main street), visit the Rector's Palace, and step inside the impressive Dubrovnik Cathedral.

Afternoon: Game of Thrones and Local Culture
For fans of Game of Thrones, a guided tour of filming locations within Dubrovnik is a must. Alternatively, take a cable car ride up to Mount Srđ for a bird's-eye view of the city and enjoy lunch with a view. If you prefer to relax, head to Banje Beach for some sunbathing and swimming.

Evening: Departure
As the ship departs, enjoy a traditional Croatian dinner onboard, reflecting on the medieval charm of Dubrovnik as it disappears from view.

Day 3: Kotor, Montenegro

Morning: Arrival and Bay of Kotor
Sail into the breathtaking Bay of Kotor, often compared to a fjord for its dramatic scenery. Upon arrival, stroll through the well-preserved medieval town of Kotor. Visit the Cathedral of Saint Tryphon and explore the maze of narrow streets filled with shops and cafes.

Afternoon: Climbing the City Walls or Coastal Excursion
For the adventurous, climb the steep steps to the Kotor Fortress for unparalleled views of the bay. Alternatively, take an excursion to the charming coastal village of Perast and visit the island of Our Lady of the Rocks, a man-made islet with a beautiful church.

Evening: Departure

Return to the ship for a relaxing evening, with the beauty of Montenegro fresh in your mind. Enjoy a local Montenegrin dish onboard, such as Njeguški pršut (smoked ham) or black risotto.

Day 4: Corfu, Greece

Morning: Arrival and Old Town
Arrive in Corfu, an island rich in history and natural beauty. Start your day exploring Corfu Old Town, a UNESCO World Heritage site. Wander through the Liston Promenade, visit the Old Fortress, and admire the Saint Spyridon Church.

Afternoon: Beaches and Monasteries
After a morning of cultural exploration, head to one of Corfu's stunning beaches such as Paleokastritsa or Glyfada for some relaxation. Alternatively, visit the Monastery of Paleokastritsa for a mix of history, spirituality, and breathtaking views.

Evening: Departure
As the ship departs Corfu, enjoy a traditional Greek dinner onboard. Try local dishes like moussaka, souvlaki, or baklava for dessert.

Day 5: Santorini, Greece

Morning: Arrival and Iconic Views
Santorini's famous caldera and white-washed buildings welcome you as you arrive. Take a trip to the island and start your day with a visit to the clifftop village of Oia,

where you'll find the island's most iconic views and photo opportunities.

Afternoon: Wineries and Beaches
After soaking in the beauty of Oia, head to a local winery to sample Santorini's unique volcanic wines, such as Assyrtiko. If time permits, relax on one of Santorini's unique beaches, like the Red Beach or Kamari Beach, known for its black sand.

Evening: Departure and Sunset
Return to the ship in time for sunset, one of Santorini's most celebrated features. Watch the sun dip below the horizon as you sail away, enjoying the romantic atmosphere of this unforgettable island.

Day 6: Mykonos, Greece

Morning: Arrival and Town Exploration
Mykonos, known for its lively nightlife and picturesque town, is your next stop. Begin with a walk through Mykonos Town (Chora), exploring the narrow streets, the iconic windmills, and the Little Venice area, where buildings hang over the water.

Afternoon: Beaches and Island Adventures
Spend the afternoon at one of Mykonos's famous beaches, such as Paradise Beach for a party vibe or Ornos Beach for a more relaxed atmosphere. If you're interested in history, take a boat trip to the nearby island of Delos, an important archaeological site.

Evening: Departure

As the sun sets, enjoy dinner onboard, reflecting on the charm and energy of Mykonos. Prepare for an exciting day in Athens tomorrow.

Day 7: Athens (Piraeus), Greece

Morning: Arrival and Ancient Wonders
Dock in the port of Piraeus, the gateway to Athens. Head straight to the Acropolis, where you can explore the Parthenon, the Erechtheion, and the Temple of Athena Nike. Visit the Acropolis Museum for a deeper understanding of these ancient sites.

Afternoon: Modern Athens
After a morning of ancient history, explore modern Athens. Visit the Plaka district for lunch and shopping, stroll through Monastiraki Square, and see the changing of the guard at Syntagma Square. If time permits, visit the National Archaeological Museum.

Evening: Departure
Return to the ship and enjoy your evening as you sail away from the cradle of Western civilization. Dine on traditional Greek cuisine and take in the last views of Athens as you set sail for Turkey.

Day 8: Kusadasi (Ephesus), Turkey

Morning: Arrival and Ephesus Exploration
Kusadasi is your gateway to the ancient city of Ephesus, one of the best-preserved Roman cities in the world. Start your day with a guided tour of Ephesus, visiting the

Library of Celsus, the Great Theatre, and the Temple of Hadrian.

Afternoon: Local Crafts and Culinary Delights
After exploring Ephesus, head back to Kusadasi for lunch. Try traditional Turkish dishes such as kebabs, meze, or baklava. Spend the afternoon browsing the local markets for Turkish carpets, ceramics, and other crafts.

Evening: Departure
As you depart from Kusadasi, enjoy the stunning views of the Aegean Sea and reflect on the incredible history you've just experienced.

Day 9: Istanbul, Turkey

Morning: Arrival and Cultural Exploration
Your final port of call is Istanbul, where East meets West. Start your day with a visit to the Hagia Sophia, an architectural marvel that has served as both a church and a mosque. Next, explore the Blue Mosque and the nearby Hippodrome.

Afternoon: Palaces and Bazaars
After lunch, visit Topkapi Palace to learn about the Ottoman Empire and explore its beautiful gardens and collections. End your day with a visit to the Grand Bazaar, one of the largest and oldest covered markets in the world. Here, you can shop for everything from spices to jewelry.

Evening: Departure

As you depart Istanbul, enjoy your last night on board with a special dinner celebrating the flavors of the Mediterranean. Take in the night views of Istanbul's skyline, with its domes and minarets lit up against the dark sky.

Day 10: Return to Venice, Italy

Morning: Disembarkation

Return to Venice, where your journey began. After breakfast, disembark and either head to the airport or take some time to explore Venice further if your schedule allows. Consider a visit to Murano or Burano islands for a final taste of Venetian culture before heading home.

Afternoon: Reflecting on Your Journey

As you make your way home, reflect on the incredible experiences and memories created during your 10-day Eastern Mediterranean cruise. From ancient ruins to modern cities, from serene beaches to bustling bazaars, this journey has offered a rich tapestry of cultures, histories, and landscapes that will stay with you long after you return home.

This 10-day itinerary provides a well-rounded experience of the Eastern Mediterranean, offering a mix of history, culture, relaxation, and adventure. Whether you're a first-time cruiser or a seasoned traveler, this journey will leave you with unforgettable memories of some of the most beautiful and culturally rich destinations in the world.

.

CHAPTER 12
PRACTICAL INFORMATION

Tips for First-Time Cruisers

Embarking on your first cruise can be an exciting yet overwhelming experience. Here are some helpful tips to ensure you have a smooth and enjoyable journey.

Start by researching and choosing the right cruise line and itinerary for your interests and budget. Different cruise lines cater to different types of travelers, so find one that matches your preferences. Look into the destinations, onboard activities, and amenities offered.

When booking your cruise, consider the cabin type and location. If you're prone to seasickness, choose a cabin in the middle of the ship where there is less motion. An interior cabin can be more budget-friendly, but if you enjoy scenic views, a balcony cabin might be worth the extra cost.

Pack wisely. Bring comfortable clothing and shoes suitable for various activities, both on and off the ship. Don't forget essentials like sunscreen, a hat, and swimwear. Check if your cruise line has any dress codes for certain restaurants or events and pack accordingly. It's also a good idea to bring a small backpack or tote bag for day trips.

Arrive at your departure port a day early to avoid any last-minute travel delays. This way, you can start your cruise relaxed and without the stress of rushing to the ship. Make sure to have all necessary travel documents, such as your passport, cruise tickets, and any required visas.

On the first day, explore the ship and familiarize yourself with its layout. Attend the safety drill, which is mandatory for all passengers, and take note of emergency procedures. This will help you feel more comfortable and confident during your cruise.

Take advantage of the activities and amenities offered onboard. Cruise ships often have a wide range of entertainment options, from live shows and movies to fitness classes and spa treatments. Check the daily schedule, which is usually delivered to your cabin each evening, to plan your activities for the next day.

When it comes to dining, most cruises offer a variety of options, from casual buffets to formal dining rooms. Try to experience different restaurants and cuisines. If you have dietary restrictions or preferences, inform the cruise staff in advance so they can accommodate your needs.

Plan your shore excursions wisely. Research the ports of call and decide which activities or sights you want to experience. You can book excursions through the cruise line or independently. Booking through the cruise line can be more convenient, but it's often cheaper to arrange your own tours. Just make sure you return to the ship on time, as it won't wait for late passengers.

Stay connected with the cruise staff and fellow passengers. They can provide valuable tips and recommendations to enhance your experience. Don't hesitate to ask questions or seek assistance if needed.

Keep track of your spending. Cruises often have additional costs for things like drinks, specialty dining, and shore excursions. Set a budget and monitor your expenses to avoid any surprises at the end of your trip.

Relax and enjoy your cruise. Take the time to unwind, meet new people, and create lasting memories. Whether you're lounging by the pool, exploring a new city, or enjoying a delicious meal, savor every moment of your first cruise adventure.

Health and Safety

Staying healthy and safe while traveling is essential to enjoying your trip to the Middle East. Here are some practical tips to help you stay well and secure during your journey.

First, it's important to be aware of the local healthcare system. Before you travel, check if your health insurance covers international travel or consider purchasing travel insurance that includes medical coverage. This ensures you have access to medical care if needed. Carry a list of emergency contacts, including local emergency numbers and the nearest embassy or consulate.

Staying hydrated is crucial, especially in the hot and dry climate of the Middle East. Always drink plenty of water and carry a refillable water bottle with you. Make sure to drink bottled or filtered water, and avoid ice in drinks if you're unsure of the water source. In some areas, tap water may not be safe to drink.

Protect yourself from the sun. The Middle East can be extremely sunny and hot, so use sunscreen with a high SPF, wear a hat, sunglasses, and light, breathable clothing to cover your skin. This not only helps prevent sunburn but also protects against heatstroke. Take breaks in the shade or indoors to cool down.

Be cautious with food. Enjoying local cuisine is a highlight of any trip, but be mindful of food hygiene. Eat at reputable restaurants and avoid street food that looks unhygienic. Make sure your food is thoroughly cooked and avoid raw or undercooked meats and seafood. Peel fruits and vegetables yourself if possible.

Be aware of local health risks. Some areas may have specific health concerns such as malaria or other mosquito-borne diseases. Check with a travel health clinic for recommended vaccinations and medications before your trip. Use insect repellent and wear long sleeves and pants to reduce the risk of mosquito bites.

Practice good personal hygiene. Wash your hands frequently with soap and water, especially before eating and after using the restroom. Carry hand sanitizer for times when soap and water aren't available. This helps prevent the spread of germs and keeps you healthy.

Be mindful of your surroundings and follow local safety advice. Research the safety situation in the areas you plan to visit and stay informed about any travel advisories. Avoid areas with political unrest or large demonstrations. Stick to well-lit and populated areas, especially at night.

Respect local customs and laws. The Middle East has diverse cultural and religious practices that may differ from what you're used to. Dress modestly, especially when visiting religious sites, and be aware of local laws regarding behavior and conduct. Showing respect for local customs can help you avoid misunderstandings and ensure a positive experience.

Keep your belongings secure. Petty theft can occur in tourist areas, so keep an eye on your belongings. Use a money belt or hidden pouch to carry your valuables, and be cautious with your wallet and phone. Avoid displaying expensive items and carry only what you need for the day.

Know where to get medical help. Familiarize yourself with the location of nearby hospitals, clinics, and pharmacies. If you need medication, bring enough for your trip along with a copy of your prescription. This ensures you have what you need and can obtain replacements if necessary.

Packing Tips

Packing for a trip can sometimes feel overwhelming, but with a few simple tips, you can make sure you have everything you need without overpacking. Here are some easy-to-follow packing tips to help you prepare for your travels.

Start by making a packing list. Write down everything you think you'll need for your trip, from clothes and toiletries to important documents and gadgets. This helps you stay organized and ensures you don't forget anything essential.

When it comes to clothes, think about the weather and activities you'll be doing. Pack versatile clothing that can be mixed and matched to create different outfits. Choose lightweight and breathable fabrics if you're traveling to a warm destination. Don't forget to pack a few layers for cooler evenings or air-conditioned places. A light jacket or sweater can be very useful.

Rolling your clothes instead of folding them can save space and reduce wrinkles. This method allows you to fit more items into your suitcase and keeps everything neat and tidy. For delicate items, consider using packing cubes or compression bags to keep them protected and organized.

Shoes can take up a lot of space in your luggage, so choose them wisely. Pack a comfortable pair for walking, a nicer pair for dining out or special occasions, and perhaps sandals or flip-flops for the beach or pool. Wear your bulkiest shoes on the plane to save space in your bag.

Don't forget your toiletries. Pack travel-sized bottles of shampoo, conditioner, and other essentials to save space. Many stores sell small, reusable containers that you can fill with your favorite products. Make sure all liquids are packed in a clear, resealable plastic bag to comply with airport security regulations.

A small first-aid kit can be very handy. Include basics like band-aids, pain relievers, any prescription medications you need, and hand sanitizer. This ensures you're prepared for minor health issues while traveling.

Important documents should be kept in a safe and accessible place. Carry your passport, ID, boarding passes, travel insurance, and any necessary visas in a travel wallet or a secure compartment of your bag. It's also a good idea to have digital copies of these documents stored on your phone or email in case you lose the originals.

Electronics are a big part of travel nowadays. Don't forget your phone, charger, power bank, and any other gadgets you might need. If you're traveling internationally, pack a universal adapter to ensure you can charge your devices anywhere.

Consider packing a small, foldable bag or backpack. This can be useful for day trips or as an extra bag for souvenirs and gifts you might pick up along the way.

Leave some space in your suitcase. You're likely to pick up a few items during your travels, and having extra room ensures you won't struggle to fit everything back in when it's time to head home.

By following these simple packing tips, you can ensure you have everything you need for a comfortable and enjoyable trip without the hassle of overpacking. Happy travels!

Useful Website and Apps

When planning your travels, having the right websites and apps at your fingertips can make a world of difference. They can help you book flights, find accommodations, navigate new cities, and even learn about local attractions. Here are some useful websites and apps that can enhance your travel experience.

For booking flights, Skyscanner is an excellent resource. It compares prices from various airlines and travel agencies, helping you find the best deals. The app is easy to use, allowing you to set price alerts and explore different travel dates to get the cheapest options.

Finding the perfect place to stay is made easy with Booking.com. This website offers a wide range of accommodations, from hotels and hostels to apartments and bed-and-breakfasts. You can read reviews from other travelers, see photos of the properties, and filter your search based on your preferences. The mobile app is equally user-friendly and helps you manage your bookings on the go.

When it comes to getting around, Google Maps is indispensable. It provides detailed maps, directions, and real-time traffic updates. You can also use it to find nearby restaurants, attractions, and public transportation options. The app allows you to download maps for offline use, which is particularly helpful when traveling to areas with limited internet access.

For discovering local attractions and activities, TripAdvisor is a go-to resource. It offers reviews, photos, and rankings of various sights and experiences from fellow travelers. You can also book tours and tickets directly through the site. The TripAdvisor app makes it easy to find things to do based on your interests and location.

For language assistance, Google Translate is incredibly handy. It can translate text, speech, and even images in real-time. This app is especially useful for navigating menus, signs, and conversations in foreign languages. You can also download languages for offline use, ensuring you have access to translations even without an internet connection.

Currency conversion is made simple with XE Currency. This app provides up-to-date exchange rates and allows you to convert currencies on the go. It's especially useful when traveling to multiple countries with different currencies. You can also set alerts for specific exchange rates to make the most of your money.

When it comes to dining, Yelp is a great app for finding local restaurants and cafes. It offers reviews, ratings, and photos from other diners, helping you choose the best places to eat. You can search for specific types of cuisine or see what's nearby, making it easy to find something that suits your taste.

For comprehensive travel planning, consider using TripIt. This app organizes all your travel details in one place, including flights, hotel reservations, car rentals, and activities. You can forward your confirmation emails to TripIt, and it will create a detailed itinerary for you. The app also provides real-time updates and alerts, ensuring you stay informed about any changes to your plans.

Having these websites and apps on hand can greatly enhance your travel experience, making it easier to plan, navigate, and enjoy your trip. They provide valuable information and tools that help you make the most of your time, ensuring a smoother and more enjoyable journey.

CONCLUSION

As we reach the conclusion of your Mediterranean travel guide, it's clear that the journey through this enchanting region is nothing short of magical. The Mediterranean, with its sun-drenched coastlines, rich history, diverse cultures, and culinary delights, offers an experience like no other. Each destination, from the bustling ports to the serene beaches, has its own unique charm and story to tell.

Traveling through the Mediterranean means immersing yourself in a tapestry of experiences. It's about wandering through ancient ruins in Greece, savoring the exquisite flavors of Italian cuisine, exploring the vibrant markets of Turkey, and basking in the natural beauty of Croatia's coastline. The Mediterranean Sea, a timeless witness to countless civilizations, continues to be a source of inspiration and wonder.

One of the most remarkable aspects of the Mediterranean is its ability to offer something for every type of traveler. Whether you're an adventurer seeking thrilling outdoor activities, a history buff eager to explore centuries-old landmarks, a foodie excited to taste local delicacies, or someone simply looking to relax on beautiful beaches, the Mediterranean welcomes you with open arms.

This travel guide has aimed to provide you with insights and recommendations to help you make the most of your Mediterranean adventure. From practical tips on currency and language to detailed guides on attractions and activities, every page has been crafted to enhance your travel experience.

As you set off on your Mediterranean journey, remember to embrace the spontaneity and serendipity that travel often brings. Some of the most memorable experiences come from unexpected encounters and unplanned detours. Allow yourself to get lost in the winding streets of charming villages, strike up conversations with locals, and savor every moment of your trip.

In conclusion, the Mediterranean is more than just a travel destination; it's a vibrant mosaic of cultures, histories, and landscapes that beckon you to explore and discover. May this guide serve as your companion, helping you navigate the wonders of the Mediterranean and create memories that will last a lifetime. Safe travels and may your Mediterranean adventure be filled with joy, discovery, and unforgettable experiences.

MAP

Scan QR Code with device to view map for easy navigation

Made in the USA
Monee, IL
20 October 2024

68256354R00115